Bureaucracitis

JJ Suff

Published by JJ Suff, 2023.

While every precaution has been taken in the preparation of this book, the publisher assumes no responsibility for errors or omissions, or for damages resulting from the use of the information contained herein.

BUREAUCRACITIS

First edition. March 20, 2023.

Copyright © 2023 JJ Suff.

ISBN: 979-8215029534

Written by JJ Suff.

Table of Contents

This book is dedicated to the Tunnel-2-Towers Foundation and the First Responders, Gold Star Military Families, catastrophically injured Veterans, and Homeless Veterans, they support.

Note the views expressed herein are solely those of the author and are not intended in any way to represent the views of the Tunnel-2-Towers Foundation, or anyone else's views within the United States Department of Defense, past or present.

Prologue

The Magic Markers in my desk, and White-Out used for typos back then, were tempting me. Could I paint eyes on the lenses of some reading glasses to make it look like I was awake and alert, while enjoying some sweet slumber? It had crossed my mind, especially when hungover, in my new job as an intern within the vast U.S. Department of Defense bureaucracy. I was convinced the clock repeatedly stopped as I ran out of ways to look occupied.

My most useful job skill seemed to be getting really good at daydreaming most of the day; women, sports, my weekend and vacation planning, all with a gigantic federal regulation open on my desk, sometimes with assorted sports magazines hidden inside. This was before cell phones, even before Al Gore invented the internet, and I had a lot of time on my hands without much to do.

However, it was my first actual career gig after college, the pay and benefits were very good, I liked my new co-workers and I could actually afford to go out drinking with them. I could even pay for better dates than romantic Taco Bell lunches, a valuable historic first in my life back then.

When I did finally get something to do here and there, it didn't seem like I was really doing anything. My alleged job was someone handing me a document supporting one step among many in a new Department of Defense purchase, critiquing it in my current review office assignment while not understanding it much, sending it to other review offices for their take, and sending it back with consolidated changes to the poor soul who prepared it and had to maybe get something done eventually.

The entire office I was in "did" that and only that, including a full staff, middle managers, and a lead manager, and was just one of many similar large offices, within many similar large DoD organizations involved in what was required to at some point buy something for the military.

I didn't realize it at the time, but looking back I believe the seeds for this book were sewn back then when I began my career in Federal Service, which my Homies and I later dubbed the white collar welfare state of Club Fed, back in early 1989.

I had entered DoD Civil Service with a lot of respect and appreciation for the U.S. Military in no small part due to being from a family with significant experience in it. So I automatically saw it as the civilian employee machine behind DoD had to be impressive too. Certainly every regulation and procedure had to be mission critical, every one of the many hundreds of thousands of civilian jobs supporting it was needed. The very best, most professional military in the world surely had the smartest and most efficient practices and people behind it.

Early on I tried to take the blue pill path of ignorance like in the original *Matrix* movie, wanting to believe it was all absolutely real, just and necessary. Maybe deep down I thought I'd be happier that way, believing in it all and finding purpose in sitting there doing my part which was therefore essential to our nation's defense, along with all the other remarkably complex parts.

Yet it kept eating at me, the better part of a million similar civilian jobs in DoD alone, and about as many more contracted civilians, altogether more than the active duty troops had. All of us civilians were navigating a colossal and chaotic labyrinth of rules and procedures to do most anything, even just to buy something now and then like my job was supposed to support.

Meanwhile the troops put their lives on the line for the rest of us, and the supplies and services we bought for them came from the private sector. We were in between, with what seemed like more people and pay than they had, or at least way more than the soldiers were paid.

We were compensated very well whether or not any real result could be identified from our roles, whereas the troops got paid much less for risking their all. The private sector companies we dealt with only got paid if they reached a clear result, by producing and delivering an actual product or service the military needed for its mission.

It dawned on me eventually that my first real career job might not be as real as I thought, maybe even mostly fake, and now I'm here to tell you that countless mostly fake, or at least questionable federal jobs, should be real news. They cost the nation huge fortunes and no one, not the military my positions were to support, or the taxpayer, gets all that much out of them. At least not nearly enough for what it costs everyone. It almost seems like the remarkable numbers of federal civilian positions are decided upon first, then incredibly vast and complex processes are invented to serve as the need for all the jobs, with little consideration for tangible, let alone cost-effective, results.

Sure there's waste, even some major waste, in the private sector too, as former President Obama correctly pointed out one time. But the distinction I believe is in nearly all cases, we have choices in what we decide to spend our money on, there's still legitimate competition for most everything else. The private company can only waste so much and expect to be successful, or even survive, since we can buy from someone else if their asking price is no longer worth it to us. For instance, *what the cluck, Egg-Land's Best?* I'll find more affordable alternatives, hell at this rate I'll be making room for a chicken coop in my basement.

However, in paying for our Federal workforce we have no other option, it's not an asking price. We must pay for every bit of it, our taxes consuming a very high portion of our incomes, stunning debt also on us beyond the annual remarkable spending, crushing our life savings, and the unintended but equally expensive consequences such as soaring inflation in more recent times. Getting our money's worth in return doesn't seem to be in the equation.

Indeed, if this gets out there to a substantial degree, one can expect possibly dismissive or even angry reactions from some. But no worries, Homies. We're all in this together; this is not an anti-government book at all. We clearly need good government practices, and therefore resources that serve the people. It only makes sense that the people contribute to everyday necessities like police, fire, and schools as some local and state level examples, and needs across the nation as a whole like a strong military, federal law enforcement, and the U.S. Postal Service.

At least a small part of my duties actually did support the military; I sincerely took pride in the maybe 10% of it that mattered. Clearly significant numbers of Federal Government civilian jobs, or at least parts of their jobs, are necessary. Just maybe not a relatively alarming percentage of our entire nation's working population.

So this book is pro-government, but could be better characterized as pro-competent government. Most of us know, regardless of our politics, that competency and accountability in government is sorely lacking to say the least, it has been for a long time, and it's definitely been a bipartisan failure. Obviously I'm a fiscal conservative, but both sides of the aisle have contributed plenty to the giant mess the Federal Government has become. A government we all serve in many ways, instead of one that serves us.

Unlike my experience in the giant tangled bureaucracies of Club Fed, I'll try to keep this book relatively organized. The first chapters will provide some perspective on just how striking the Club's condition is including what I submit are some funny and intriguing possible causes, then the impact of its collective madness on you (you might want to pour a strong Old Fashioned before that one). After that I will offer some possible solutions, at least to the part I was in for over three decades, plus some suggested coping strategies for my fellow civil servants and I hope anyone else working in huge bureaucracies.

I sure don't have the full solution, the fixes to the whole incredible and complex state of chaos the Club seems to be in. Yet what I will humbly offer could help the Fed scene work better, even save the nation hundreds of billions in no time, to either put back in the pockets of the people, or use towards more useful projects that serve the people. I think the savings might even be able to fund an electric vehicle for every household, or at least a widespread booze voucher program. I bet America might unite behind that one right about now.

Also, I sure don't want anyone hurt by writing this book. All names are changed to protect the guilty, specific DoD offices and other organizations not revealed, either. I'll always see fellow civil servants as my teammates, a strange but valued Fraternity of Futility seemed to exist amongst us. Plus despite my battles with the establishment many times, I still very much appreciate how truly good it was to me over the years. I was also extra lucky no one seemed to get fired at the Club.

Finally, as a form of public service and support to the military which I didn't do well enough at over my career, at least 50% of the author's proceeds for every copy of this book sold will be donated to the Tunnel-2-Towers Foundation, my favorite cause in retirement. How that will be accounted for is explained at the end of the book. The rest of the royalties I'll need since life in America, including Taco Bell lunches and drinking with my friends, has become a lot more expensive these days. *JJ Suff*

Chapter 1
A Random Day of Dysfunction

"The work is fake, but the check is real."

Anonymous Club Fed Philosopher, Circa 2013

So what's it like day to day in the so-called white collar welfare state sometimes also known as Club Fed? Moreover, are there clear, consistent results which benefit you as a taxpayer? Let me share a realistic depiction of most of my days at the Club and you decide. Later on we'll get into what it adds up to in terms of its bigger impact and costs considering just how huge the Club really is; how many gigs are more or less like mine was, and how many more surround them that may be more questionable.

<u>05:50 am</u>

I arrive at my cubicle early as usual, hoping to get the tangled cluster of DoD IT systems up and running to start my day, which can often take an hour or more. DoD may spend more millions per capita on its numerous IT systems than anyone, and I wonder if we could fund the Green New Deal if we ever got our shit together. There are over 15 different and involved online tools to use in my buying job and they don't get along well together, plus a bunch of other systems everyone used.

I have over 20 logins and passwords, and a Common Access Card (CAC) though I don't understand what is meant by the Common Access part. But it's a better beginning than many days, my emails start pouring in by 06:15 am and I struggle with my EAD, Email Anxiety Disorder, knowing it's going to be another interesting day. Ten emails pop, then 20, 40...50...

After my earliest years I was dumb enough to end up in gigs that were a sort of production by Club Fed standards, originating most of the documents that the rest of the establishment, the majority of it, utilized to say they do something; various touches like signatures along the way, reviews, audits, ample lanes and layers of micromanagers... It brought lots of emails beyond the usual volumes of garbage that everyone got. Among them are urgent demands to complete huge spreadsheets answering to the perceived failings in my documents. One new Excel Apocalypse goes down to Row 132 and out to Column AY. Shit.

<u>06:30 am</u>

Letch storms into my cube for his typical morning rant, interrupting my initial email efforts. He got his nickname by spending most of his work hours trolling for a young foreign bride online, VISA card always at the ready. Maybe Letch was prophetic too, since he kindly tried to free a number of young girls from Ukraine's oppression long before Vladimir Putin did. He's a very proud public servant, convinced everyone but him in our office is a blithering idiot. He wears a Dallas Cowboys jacket, hat and gaudy team belt buckle but can't name a single current player, at most maybe a few from the 1990s. As a dedicated football fan I find that reprehensible.

Letch hates the place with a passion, though the odds of him holding down a decent paying job anywhere else have to be near zero. When he's not surfing for child brides, he occasionally generates some utterly incoherent paperwork for me to fix and sign, then enter into the massive review and audit gauntlets to answer to, along with my own.

He says our agency mismanagement should all be fired immediately, and asks me why the Republican Party, the root of all evil in the universe, should not all be in federal prison. The last part is to get a rise out of me, he knows I lean conservative, but as always I don't take the bait and tell him both major parties absolutely suck. I mean it too.

Letch has no answer to that and mercifully my buddy Dante gives me a Remote Rescue - overhearing the rant he calls me to discuss fantasy football. Letch glares at me bewildered and agitated a while since I don't end the call. Then he finally leaves to check if he got a reply from another marriage prospect, this time a lost orphan girl in Vietnam.

<u>07:05 am</u>

My first line supervisor Sam stops by, he's a good guy I like but nervously tells me "we" need to get the largest Excel Apocalypse answered by noon, or our Rulers will be upset. I start to sweat some, the documents in question are almost all pretend, the perceived failings in them even more imagined, and the pressing deadline is arbitrary too. But plenty in Club Fed believe it's real, serious, and urgent. Shit.

After my screening of the 57 morning emails, quickly dumping what I can, I dive in to answer my many alleged documentation errors, which also includes diving, spelunking is more like it, into the massive ever-changing labyrinth of regulations and procedures to try to understand where my critics are coming from.

There are many thousands of pages of regulations, procedures, manuals, etc., across dozens of different streams and layers, and they are changed continually to help us paperwork Minions maintain high compliance. Even just the three most major sets of regulations total over 4,000 pages of detailed coverage, including over 1,000 eligible clauses for the contracts we try to place. A team of eight bureaucrats from Headquarters were in on the gargantuan spreadsheet, it took them weeks. I have 48 hours to answer, with just over 4 hours left...

<u>07:30 am</u>

Damnit here comes The Fossil. Another angry guy whose documents I try to fix and sign, and he too needs to vent about our dysfunctional scene this morning. The Fossil is ancient, I wonder how old he actually is. He looks and sounds even older than our past two Presidents, resembling a pale, fossilized Grinch. So is he 90, 95? His dentures, denture is more like it, is a continuous caked in yellowish mass, like a single flat super wide tooth, maybe a filthy antique plastic hairband crammed onto his drooling top gums. He first wore today's polyester three-piece suit back when Jimmy Carter was inaugurated.

Why should The Fossil retire though? He has nothing else in his life, his make-work is actually mine, and the pay and bennies are great. He starts out with a simmering anger but it builds into a tirade, his spittle flying onto my keyboard. Then he storms off to email the local Federal Employee Union about his grievances, and I wonder if and when his furious pounding of a keyboard near me will someday cease, and after a wait I'll arrive to find his cold corpse, stiff fingers left on the keys spelling out his last expletives. I'm ashamed of myself wondering if part of me longs for that day.

Just like Letch, The Fossil rails on the crimes and horrors of big government while voting for more of it, he even actively campaigns for it. It's one of the many mysteries of the Club I ponder at times, though I really need to complete that giant spreadsheet this morning, and I'm also put on notice that one of my over 40 mostly pretend annual online courses to help me lead a safer life, and be a better employee, is overdue. If not done by the end of the day I will let down the whole team and we won't get to leave an hour early before our next holiday off. Even worse, the course emphasizes climbing stairs safely and I'll face imminent peril before I tackle the next stairwell if I don't get it done. Shit.

<u>08:10 am</u>

I'm feeling stressed and need a break with my Homies downstairs in the very well-equipped Club Fed fitness center. I should probably get some sauna or massage time there to feel better too, but I never take advantage of those perks since that'd be wrong. I know my anxiety shouldn't be there, none of what drives it is truly real. But I can't help it, and some laughs and comradery with my friends will get me back on track. As usual I exercise very little and mainly shoot the shit a while, though I know I need to get back to getting busy in my cubicle.

Back to it by 08:40 am, I bounce back and forth from spreadsheet minutia to my cascading emails. A new message admonishes me for a single code in a form block being a digit off. The woman who sent it studies and signs one form a week then reports on it, and she's very thorough. The rest of the time she's an FA, Facebook Analyst, like plenty of others in our establishment. Those of us Minions who must produce the documents for everyone else truly can't stand her.

Another email demands contact info for the culture office of a contractor I support an equipment maintenance contract with, claiming their employees have a poor attitude. I reply that the small business firm repairs equipment at military bases and doesn't have such offices.

They also don't have multiple analysis offices, morale offices, transformation offices, inclusivity offices, or other large well-staffed offices that we have, either. They'd go bankrupt if they did. But I don't mention those. I do let her know we have not figured out a way to pay the contractor in our methods for months, which could conceivably be impacting their attitude. They don't get paid no matter what every two weeks like we do, succeeding in spite of ourselves, but I don't mention that part either.

<u>09:30 am</u>

Progress has been made, the spreadsheet exercise may get close enough to send onward before lunch, the email circus no worse than usual. But trying to spend some of your money on a supply order in our systems gets met with just a spinning dial on the screen each time. No problem, I let it spin and tend to my other tasks to defend our nation. When the ordering try times out I just try it again and again. I'm killing it this morning!

Jackie stops by about 09:45. I like her, she's smart, funny and among those of us who didn't take the blue pill in the Matrix. We bond by making the best of it though, which of course focuses on making fun of it. She recently started using the term "Clownage" for our scene. It stuck. She tells me about her weekend, including a demo which includes her bending over rocking her hips, large boobs bouncing and long blonde hair flying around. I'm very distracted, also nervous, since my wife works in a nearby group of cubicles. Jackie looks at a work email on her phone and has to leave, muttering *"Oh' the fucking clownage, the buffoonery..."* on her way out.

<u>10:20 am</u>

Giving up on the stuck system to obligate more of your money onto a DoD contract so the private sector can get us something we need, I instead turn my multi-tasking efforts to streaming my fake class that's due, while still working the spreadsheet and emails. They've adjusted the class like they have others, I have to engage it at least a little to keep it moving along, and it eventually gets done. Whew, I can safely climb stairs again! I see that my next class due after this one is a newer one about extremists in DoD, and I wonder if it may instead be required by the actual extremists in DoD.

I'm getting anxious again because my buddies and I like to leave early for lunch so it looks like we're not gone too long. I commit to forwarding the spreadsheet by 10:55 including some cells I know will be lacking, but I can claim I met the deadline and handle those in my first round of revisions. I turn down an offer from some other teammates to join them for a lunch and learn session on meditation techniques to cope with the increasing job stress we've all been facing. Two open positions in our buying arena haven't been filled for months, that's at least a few forms or a checklist a week put on the rest of us, considering the two jobs involved. So wrong.

11:05 am

I made it, lunch time at last, after I sent the spreadsheet onward into the approval gauntlet. Dante, another buddy Roberto, and I embark for lunch, bitching about various proud fools we answer to in the bureaucracy, our controlling wives, and our fantasy football teams. The usual, but we enjoy it over sub sandwiches, opting not to go somewhere for drinks instead. It's been known to happen. We are experienced drinkers, never careless enough to raise suspicion, but some real amateurs in the office got out of hand too many times and ruined it for everyone. There was a big crackdown by our Rulers. The higher level Ruler who dramatically announced the possible consequences after lunch one day sounded pretty drunk when he gave the slurred speech.

<u>12:15 pm</u>

I'm back in the game, keyboard on fire in the cube, the arrival time looking like we were just a little late from our supposed 11:30 am to noon half hour lunch. My immediate boss Sam is a good guy, we don't see him as a Ruler and he may have been on a 2 hour lunch, anyway. A prior boss I had, a devoted Ruler, would tell me to take 15 minutes of leave or work over if I was 6 minutes late from lunch, the only thing he did as a highly effective DoD leader. It was really irritating; he'd literally be holding the 300 copies of his church bulletin he'd just made on the office copier, when he'd bust me.

I try to place that supply order again, and again no luck. Can't I at least buy a couple pieces of equipment for DoD today? Getting the contract in place for them sure was an undertaking, it'd be great to get something from it. I wonder if it was easier to launch Obamacare than it was to place that broad long term contract and others like it. I did manage to get it awarded well under the 12 to 24 month timeframe many other contracts like it took in our practices, however.

We're just buying routine things too, so I wonder what an aircraft carrier acquisition must be like. It'd seem we'd have to start it before the aircraft carrier was even invented, or maybe before ships were.

Come to think of it, I need my own supply item so I make a note to launch the process of requesting an ergonomic assessment of my office chair, a new one would be a lot more comfortable and stress relieving. Back to my emails, more people are bitching about contractors we refuse to pay...

1:10 pm

Time for another break, this day has been tiring. I see my Homies in the fitness center again. I really like them, they are always cheerful, and one young recruit there seems so smart and capable I tell her she'd better get the hell out of Club Fed before it's too late. My theory has always been after 10 years it's over, the alternate reality becomes one's entire reality. It'd be too difficult to transition to where you must reach a clear result to get paid.

I keep this break shorter, feeling guilty, and am back at it in my cubicle by 1:35 pm. Less than 90 minutes left and I call it a day! One new email resurrects an old challenge for its large cross-functional team involved – literally one cent has not been accounted for under its contract from 14 years ago. I'm not alone in seeing it as WPJW, Way-Past-Just-Wow, a couple others in the ancient email threads also bravely pointed out the sheer absurdity and likely costs of this exercise intermittently revisited over the years. Accounting for that penny was possibly into the many tens if not hundreds of thousands of dollars by now.

However, no price is too high to show we're accountable to the taxpayer. The dedicated Rulers involved, led by a pompous guy from finance known as The Worm, insist we won't be audit ready without finding a way to fully address that penny, long ago lost when the past buying system was brought offline and its replacement launched.

<u>2:15 pm</u>

I realize The Fossil has been unusually quiet this afternoon, no outbursts, his keyboard silent, nothing. Uh' oh', could this be the day? I feel obligated to check on him. He's in his cube, motionless, head slumped forward, his crusty yellow hairband denture is almost bone dry on the desk, just some crystallizing drool. Not a good sign, it's been out a long time. I lean in, I have to...and finally hear quiet snoring, just a slight wheeze from one nostril. He sure looks like a cadaver though, each day brings him closer. But it wouldn't matter even if he snored like a drunken Wildebeest. When this has happened before everyone pretends not to notice, even any Rulers who walk by. It's better this way.

On the way back to my desk I see Letch intently studying his monitor screen while clutching his cell phone excitedly. From a distance at least, it looks like a map of Southeast Asia. It's better this way too.

<u>2:25 pm</u>

I try to order that equipment one last time, the system still spins in perpetuity, and I give up, knowing I really tried, also submitting a trouble ticket on it. I expect the response will refer to a broad systemic problem being worked so the ticket is immediately closed while asking me to complete a survey on how well they resolved my problem. That turns out to be correct.

At least my email has been working well all day. When that went down we'd find out it was a broad system problem only after it was back up, via an email message letting us know it had gone down, and the projected resolution timeframe which had passed.

Around 2:30 pm Sam visits again, as mentioned a good natured guy and he grins as he points out some spreadsheet responses where I more or less tell the auditors the underlying premise that our methods are functional, is utterly preposterous. This really is true when everything is always wrong according to something or someone out there in the vast DoD and Federal chaos of hoops and its unlimited interpretations. But I confess I was just buying time and will adjust those by tomorrow. He really needs them today so I agree to revise the spreadsheet to be more acceptable before I leave.

On his way out he tells me he was admonished by a High Ruler this morning, for not showing up at a leadership teamwork exercise coloring posters with crayons. The Ruler practically called it an Insurrection, another January 6th, not supporting something that critical to the Club's mission and democracy. Sam and I agreed that developing crayon skills at a young age can eventually pay off big, helping punch one's ticket for high level DoD Ruler positions.

More emails keep popping, many claim to be urgent such as a new one reminding us again to use the latest revision of a certain form, though the total number of potential forms to use in our gigs seems to stretch to infinity and beyond, and they are always changing. One time I started counting them for the entertainment value and stopped at 400.

<u>3:10 pm</u>

I did it! Needed a little more time to send the spreadsheet onward again, now signing off for the day. Working over 10 minutes is just plain wrong, so I put a Post-It on the lap top reminding me to add that credit time in the morning, rounding it to 15 minutes credit. Signing off can be like signing on in our struggling DoD systems, so I do the manual power button hold for 8 seconds to get the satisfaction of seeing the power light shut down for the day.

On the drive home I reflect on my day while looking forward to a strong Old Fashioned. Like most days, I didn't manage to buy anything in my DoD buying job, or reach any true result I could identify. Nonetheless, I completed a large spreadsheet deemed critical though no one knows why, and I answered a number of emails about nothing. At least I completed a class to help me lead a safer life, had some good times with friends and teammates, and I'm paid nearly $60 an hour. I probably sort of worked, granted without accomplishing anything, for at least 3 hours, but I'm confident it was more than most in my scene. I believe a lot more. My white-collar welfare life is very good in Club Fed, and I'm grateful.

Chapter 2
The Outputs are Inputs

"Meaningless work done to perfection is still meaningless."

Origins unknown but it became a War Cry of the Minions.

The high ranking member of Congress approaches the podium proudly yet solemnly, this announcement is a biggie, a huge accomplishment indeed. Epic is more like it, as the dutifully enthused press and huge assembly of bureaucrats watch the historic moment unfold...

"Today we are sending to the President's desk, the most extraordinary legislation ever passed since the dawn of time, the Rescue the World Plan. No one has read its 11,400 pages but we passed this immediately to save the world. It will rebuild roads and bridges everywhere, save our crumbling Ivy League universities from years of neglect, protect the sovereign borders of Korruptistan, turn our moon into a giant elliptical solar panel that will beam renewable low-cost energy back to earth..."

You know the drill, and this one will cost just $7.4 trillion over the next ten years, a bargain to save the world. But that's just the input, the cost of the inputs at least. What about the output, what is actually being accomplished from the inputs? Like the toddler character remarked in the old E-Trade commercials, *"Nobody knows..."*

It really is all about the inputs, no one seems to care what output it brings, especially any accounting of it. There's almost no follow up at all down the road, no idea if the inputs were ever successful.

The government institution has done its job though, because its outputs are actually inputs.

That's exactly how my Club Fed experience went, but not so much the costs really. Yes no one seemed to care about that, we just made sure we spent everything we could so we'd get at least that much or more to spend next year.

What was more intriguing, astonishing really, was the constant proliferation of process inputs, always more and more in terms of regulation, procedure, innumerable online transactions, as if the staggering amount and complexity of inputs we already had were failing us. They weren't enough, so we needed more, but they really were the reason we were failing.

It was most often driven by what was perceived to go wrong in the documents we processed, a single legal, policy or audit concern could launch a bunch more regulation or policy. Our Rulers were often awed by lawyers, even the most inept in our legal offices, which was really saying something, more on that later. Reputable, powerful law firms don't often recruit from the Club to my knowledge.

The reaction could be launched immediately in a sense, which must sound ironic considering we're talking about government practices here. But it'd first be required via an urgent email the Minions called an FNO, a From-Now-On, then the regulation or policy change, or whole new coverage, would follow someday. Such as *"Effective immediately you must use the following statement in Block 17d of DoD Form..."* and there were hundreds of these emails each year.

There was no sense of context to it. Something very obscure, irrelevant really, the whole document didn't need to exist, it never did a year earlier, and the discovered flaw, namely if it was deemed a *"Repeat Finding"*, would launch the urgent response. It'd be a celebrated output when implemented, but it was of course another input.

Inputs were Always "In" at the Club

I didn't track it over the years but I'd say total manufactured execution and especially coordination steps in terms of all the inputs to finally buy something for the military, at least doubled in my time at the Club, though it was already staggering when I first started. So our part of the Club had to grow in terms of people for all the make-work too, nearly doubling where I had spent most of my career. Especially remarkable when the time span correlated with the greatest technological advancements ever in terms of processing information, from roughly 1990 to 2020. It was more efficient back 1990 when I'd hand a clerk typist handwritten entries onto a memo form they'd use a typewriter to prepare.

Okay I did at least draft memos and other documents much faster later on, but we kept adding more and more of them and in more detail, and more touches by others, to call them done. Then the rapidly increasing online systems with their new processes, but which mostly weren't replacing past practices deemed inefficient. The systems kept adding a myriad of new make-work steps.

Around twelve years ago, a new huge system to use, it would be most our important system but still another one of many, had over 70 sets of instructions for different steps, totaling over 10,000 pages of detailed procedure. The Minions couldn't get it to work, at least not using the massive sets of disjointed instructions, so it became an arduous trial and error journey. Only the Rulers who didn't use it knew it worked flawlessly.

Strangely I ended up liking it in many ways, I killed a lot of time trying to figure it out, looking very busy. It was always a plus when a Ruler walked by and saw me toiling away. I was pretty anti-establishment by then, and I imagined the Ruler thinking *"That Minion's an asshole, but he sure is one hard working asshole."*

The clear MO to us Minions seemed to be *"If at first you don't succeed, add shitloads more inputs in terms of added regulation, procedure, online processes..."* In fact, adding another large involved input for the same thing to happen in the end, was the greatest accomplishment, it was the most celebrated output at the Club. The most accolades, awards and advancement opportunities came to those who added the most impressive new processes, mostly in gigs surrounding the Minions.

Not always though, a Minion could volunteer to help add more inputs, be on another new team bringing us another involved process we never needed before, but would soon become be an essential practice. It could be a win for the Minions partaking, an award or maybe even help them escape Minion status someday, and get into a better surrounding gig.

The Minion's attempts to contribute to the team would usually be dismissed of course, especially if they tried to minimize the damage of the initiative. The Rulers knew that only those who didn't do the work knew how the Minions should do it. But it helped the Rulers because they could say the Minions were on board, so it obviously included appropriate working knowledge and excellent coordination.

It'd go something like this, via a grand announcement on email, or an assembly, often both for a bigger input that is seen as a really great output:

"Team, starting this June we're launching our new Document Improvement Quality System, DIQS, to help us deliver greatly improved compliance for our internal and external customers..." and the Ruler goes on to commend those who developed it while presenting them awards. The Minions in the assembly are thinking *"So this in addition to our other four processes for that same thing?"*

The answer is yes, that question of course shall not be asked. The Ruler summarizes the new added procedure, usually with a giant flowchart, screen shots of the new online exercise, and how it and of itself will also be tracked for compliance, basically how we are complying with the new compliance practice. So we needed to properly use DIQS at the Club from then on.

One time a Minion from my team signed up for one of these, and it brought me a sense of true impending doom. I'll call him Larry the Science Guy. I liked him as I did most of my teammates, but he was that guy who could turn each small step of everything into a giant leap, a major science project. Terrifying, given how many steps we faced. He'd create flowcharts to document how he created the flowcharts to back-up routine forms, each taking weeks. My boss Sam knew not to give him much to do, he only needed a little something to occupy him 40 hours a week plus lots of overtime.

This project to add even more procedure wasn't as big as many, it was to address one specific type of task only a few Minions had to do now and then, but I was one of them. It of course never before needed its own special process; there was tons of other existing coverage to apply to it, we just used that and it eventually got done somehow. Too inconsistent, our Rulers declared, so here we go again.

By that time in my life at the Club I'd learned that the more processes we added, all of them complicated, micro-precise and continually changing, the less consistency and compliance we could attain. I tried to share that thought at times, but it was of course dismissed as pure blasphemy. Clearly any idiot could see we instead needed even more complex processes.

In any case, our Minion Larry the Science guy joined the new process team, though as not such a far reaching initiative it needed just the one Minion, one policy type and a few Rulers to review and approve it. The policy types in our realm were basically more Rulers though, we served them instead of the other way around.

Plus this particular policy Ruler could magically, maniacally is more like it, also find ways to turn almost nothing into a stunningly Herculean task. She made me think of Gollum from *"Lord of the Rings"*, she looked like a bizarre ghoulish thing fondling the new manuals she'd create, repeating the phrase *"My precious...,"* while adding sadistic massive new local policies for us to follow. The only good thing was it'd usually take her at least two years at it every time.

So when Larry the Science Guy got paired with Gollum, it was absolutely the most unholy matrimony I've ever witnessed in my life, a horrifying prospect for any Minion who had to execute what they came up with. I hoped it'd take until past my projected retirement about a decade after they started, there was a good chance it would. Somehow the Rulers pressured them into putting out something in about 18 months, fast tracking the essential new process we never needed before. They both put in tons of overtime to pull it off, and got nice awards for the feat.

I was dragged into it a little here and there, not even attempting to lessen the damage in the unfolding catastrophe. What I didn't see coming is they ended up despising each other, I guess just too much alike for this to work. Both wanted to add more excruciating detail than the other, a furious competitive battle ensued, even getting ugly. *"Oh' yeah?!"* Gollum would shriek, *"You think that's thorough, Larry? I'll show you thorough, you arrogant fucking prick!"*

Who knows though, maybe when it was just those two in the conference room hammering out more minutia late into the evenings on overtime, the stress and fury would erupt into unbridled passion. They might have torn each other's clothes off and had heated sex amidst the mountains of regulations and policies they'd piled into the room as references and samples. Random pages of complex procedures and flowcharts would stick to their sweaty flesh as they rolled around in it all. Larry might kill the moment though, as he'd stop to examine the regulatory citations that had become imprinted on Gollum's ass.

I'll spare you all the rest of this one, except try to imagine developing at least 30 detailed steps to merely post a check in your checkbook. First a thorough plan to show you will comply with the required thorough procedure, getting that plan approved by at least three friends and relatives beforehand, provided their qualifications to approve it are also documented in attachments to the plan. Then follow the procedure and plan to annotate the check amount, the required pen you'd use, its ink, the size and neatness standards needed to write down the numbers.

Then the simple math, good God the simple math, it must be shown as compliant and accurate. Show it in detail, attach screen shots of your laptop's calculator with each number entered then the result, document it separately in a formal memo and get that approved by the three who approved the plan. Two separate certifications by others as well, to demonstrate the integrity of the process, one of them a Math Professor, and don't forget to attach their degrees. I could go on, since they made this analogy seem streamlined, but you get the point.

Other versions of this phenomenon occurred regularly. I remember a High Ruler calling an assembly to share what he learned while visiting another DoD institution like ours. On the screen he showed us a masterpiece to follow, the new gold standard for this particular input, a summary of an action consisting of over 200 detailed pages that repeated all the other forms and documentation in the action, and then some. It alone probably took a year.

The dumb lazy Minions in our office, especially me, had been doing that step in less than 10 pages. I think it was Jackie who first texted Dante, Roberto and I during the disturbing display; *"Someone please pass the fucking vodka..."*

Another area we got very good at was wasting fortunes in inputs to demonstrate we were not wasting fortunes, namely in the price of something we finally bought. I'm trying to keep this readable for regular people outside of the government too, so let me just say that depending on particulars, it'd be about like you spending $3,000, or even $30,000, to document in excruciating detail, and while obtaining permission from all your relatives, that you didn't get ripped off when you bought $300 worth of groceries.

Not too long before I retired, the establishment added even more documentation, but this time to show how much you did to streamline the process at the working level. What you did to save lead-time while not being allowed to save lead-time, and it needed to be formally documented. That paperwork added more review and approval time too.

One more I can't resist - my agency even claimed to reduce the massive size of its main regulation at one point, a giant supplement to higher level rules, but tons of coverage allegedly reduced was still there by hyperlinks instead, with also more surrounding agency procedures than ever. A shell game. At an assembly celebrating that great accomplishment, I did end up blurting out *"Open the hyperlinks!"* The impulsive, dumb move didn't go over well for me that day. Censoring the Minions was becoming a more common practice by then.

<u>Reviewing was the New Doing</u>

With the massive yet always growing processes and procedures, the Club had to work harder to ensure they were being followed, or we'd obviously fail miserably. We had to keep expanding the reviewing and auditing processes, the reviews and audits became the most critical input that was believed to be an output. This was of course way smarter than fixing the dysfunctional and disorganized inputs, that nonsensical notion should get no attention whatsoever. It didn't even qualify as blasphemy it was so dumb.

So the most important "work", seriously believed to be the real doing in the enterprise, was reviewing and judging what others did, namely the Minions. Though not officially Ruler jobs like management was, these Rulers were often more powerful. As mentioned earlier, these Rulers' findings could easily bring us more regulations and policies, so compliance would inevitably decline as how much to comply with grew, then more findings would create more shit to follow, and the cycle of stupid continued.

Even when the review Rulers didn't bring us more shit to try to comply with, already so much we couldn't remotely find it all, they'd just give us more shit in general, impede us from doing the make-work they also needed to say they did something. Yes I can admit not all of the feedback was foolish, no one on their own thinks of everything, including all of what might actually matter. But with so much to follow that didn't matter, just the mountains of processes to nowhere, the trivial or even clearly irrelevant usually became the show-stoppers. I'd estimate that 98 percent of what blocked us had no bearing on the real results needed from the action, or had any true risks at all.

Also, while three hopefully somewhat sane takes are better than one, thirty is not better than three if you ask me and I bet most of the other Minions. Thirty or more weighing in tends to bring in more extreme takes the groupthink therefore still tries to satisfy, impeding if not failing the result everyone needs, including the extremists whether or not they understand that. But the Rulers knew it was misguided to even consider the point of diminishing returns may arrive fairly soon, then tank as the number keeps increasing.

The most reviews I actually counted on an acquisition's make-work, in terms of number of reviews along the way but not total people, was well over 50. There were around 25 different people across that I'll admit, so I guess streamlined by some Club standards. This was a routine action too, something we'd done repeatedly for decades, not say a high-tech missile program deal. Also, I forgot to count multiple after action audits much later on. I bet there were at least 10 more feasting on it later, so call it over 60 total reviews from experts in what they don't do.

Part of the dysfunction was a commitment to putting those who knew the least, into the powerful review Ruler gigs where people should know the most. Maybe not too surprising, though, since it's believed to be prudent to have powerful Cabinet Secretaries leading what they show no evidence of having knowledge and experience in. Anyway, it makes sense to have at least legal reviews on some actions for sure, it's a litigation happy America as we all know. But when they had no meaningful experience in what they were looking at, and were very nervous in general because of it, there were so many roadblocks the whole city would grind to a halt.

The legal Rulers, and plenty of policy Rulers as well, would be scared, even terrified if they perceived, or imagined, most any problem at all, which our methods guaranteed anyway. The problems were almost always something trivial from a manufactured rule or policy, not something with actual risks like a contractor being financially harmed by our incompetence. We did that a lot of course, but it almost never became a legal problem, and the risk of that was rarely noticed since we focused on the trivial or irrelevant instead.

Some of the battles were legendary; we'd practically be begging to be allowed to finally do something. I'd be desperately pointing out that I'd be signing the shit anyway, not them, and I'd be the fall guy in the extremely unlikely even it went seriously wrong. Not good enough, they didn't want to be even remotely associated with a small perceived infraction, even if imagined, an interpretation issue every time. The management Rulers, especially at higher levels, usually backed the review Rulers because they were easily scared too, also in no small part due to not knowing much in many if not most cases, not having the hands on experience that brings context too. The very highest Rulers, brave leaders all, were good at using *"I concur if everyone else does..."* and wouldn't give us much more than that.

We ended up having to manipulate these situations to finally get something done here or there. Very often there'd be no official support of an action, everyone was afraid to. But lanes and Rulers would be afraid to clearly be the one to block it either, since that also could get them in trouble. In their minds anyway, I never saw it happen but it still seemed to provide some leverage.

So we learned to frame things such that no clearly explained illegalities or major policy failures provided by a certain date, other than maybe some waffling commentary we'd get back, would let us execute, usually with some changes so people felt like they did something. A strange truce sort of developed, and it mostly worked. If the action was believed to go badly later, they could show they never did concur with it really. But they didn't stop it either, if that had backfired. You could call it leveraging the fear I guess.

Incidentally, I did have a few dealings with the esteemed U.S. Government Accountability Office, GAO, among our reviewing and judging Rulers, which would strike absolute fear and panic in my High Rulers when those times arose. Congress could even learn of our local office's incompetence if these instances went wrongly enough (not that we could match Capitol Hill's incompetence). Yet these occasions were not too bad in my experience, other than one all-star who demanded why I didn't document and file the qualifications of each bureaucrat signing a bunch of Government Inspection Reports, despite their titles shown in the paperwork. I wanted to ask him what his qualifications were to be a GAO Attorney, since it seemed his only degree might be a new Club form of an MBA - a Master of Being an Asshole.

The other occurrences were okay though. One time I shared with a GAO Team that we really did have tens of thousands of disorganized, changing rules to follow, and somehow interpret as many judges would later, and that the system can't conceivably work. There was a stunned, confused look from a couple of them, and they actually asked me to explain further. So I did, and they took it well I thought, just astounded by it really. Nothing came of it of course, but they were decent to deal with, and I was thankful for them compared to plenty of other judges we faced.

I could write another book on just that shit, but I don't want to lose your attention, dear reader. Let me leave that thought just by sharing how badly us Minions wanted to get into those gigs, the policy Ruler ones at least, since most of us did not have legal degrees. We'd be set forever, could do no wrong, only the Minions, namely the Minions who signed the make-work, got the serious critique. We alone were judged and faced consequences, though thankfully most of those were silly, one of the many benefits we found in the swirling sea of ineptitude. Yet only we were scored on the whole dysfunctional establishment really, since everything and everyone else by definition couldn't possibly be why anything went wrong.

One time I got a bootleg email I wasn't supposed to see. It was about why I was passed up for one of those sweet gigs. It was complimentary in a sense, but still funny and very revealing. The gist of it was we need that Minion and the others like him to keep producing the most make-work the rest of us need, not judging it. Besides, that poor dumb ass in particular keeps getting hung up on why we can do something instead of why we can't.

Maybe to better cover the phenomena of the outputs actually being inputs, think of a poker game, let's call it...

"Beltway Hold 'Em"

The celebrated output that is instead just another process input starts with the legislation itself, what Congress passes, which we know is always a follow-the-money process. There are lots of lobbyists from all kinds of donors and special interests, political pressures including the agenda of whoever is in power, huge slabs of pork for Congressional Districts, you know the drill so I won't elaborate further. It gets big and complicated in a hurry though.

That's the first bet of inputs, a big pile of chips that gets pushed into the middle of the table, an impressive piece of legislation covering how we must buy things for the Federal Government, or in this case let's just say some major changes to it, including more socioeconomic goals, for example.

The next player is the legions of bureaucrats who create the Federal level regulations. They need to prove their worth, their implementation regulations become massive and involved quickly, since the legislation itself is. It's time to impress here, show the thoroughness, rules covering how everything should be closely controlled so it will be more successful at reaching the goals of the legislation, what the bribery is trying to attain.

So they don't just match the first bet, they raise it, a bunch more input chips get pushed into the pile. Their bet is way bigger than it needs to be, but that's how this works. It's ballsy really, in a messed up government sort of way, already upping the ante that much.

Then it's DoD's turn. Not to be outdone, it's the U.S. Department of Defense we're talking about for God's sake, no wimps here. They sure aren't going to fold, and no way are they just going to match what's been bet, operate with just those rules. They up the ante too, but not by as much, maybe some of them are already getting pretty nervous about how much longer it will take to buy something the troops need. They add implementing regulations to the implementing regulations, but not that all that much really, not by Club Fed standards at least.

But the pile of chips being bet is already turning into a huge shitload.

Then it's my DoD Agency's turn. Uh' oh', their power players, my High Rulers, don't see it quite like DoD does. It's time to really impress here, many of them aspire to move up to DoD level gigs, they must show their regulations implementing the implementing regulations already developed, will control things even better.

They stun all the players with how much they raise the stakes, a big pile of chips gets added on.

Now everyone is getting really nervous, what is the last player going to do? It's the activities of the agency, the offices that are the front lines in the Club Fed scene, where the make-work actually happens. They need to still get something sort of done at some point, the closest anyone gets to a true output, actually buying something, so contractors can then still do the most by producing and delivering it. Can this Beltway Hold 'Em player really risk it all then, raising the stakes even more?

There's a pause, maybe my home team suddenly had reservations about adding more, raising the bet way higher still, which would be tough to fathom there was already so much. It was a ruse though, our player was just messing with everyone, their sly poker face breaking into a big grin...

You bet they raise the bet, they raise it with a bunch more inputs. They need to show they'll control the Minions even better than the agency's impressive bet, and everyone else's.

Some of our High Rulers also aspire to go higher, at least to Agency level, this is a great way to do it. They have the best people to do it too, people who know how to get things done like Larry the Science Guy, Gollum, plenty of local Rulers who are experts in what they don't ever have to execute.

Everyone is stunned by the mountain of chips at the end, the players can't see each other across it. An eerie silence ensues, it lasts a long time. Deep down, some have to realize this can't be executed, at least not on time, definitely not with high compliance either. But no one understands that part, or that it costs even more fortunes.

It's not their problem though, the Minions are who needs to execute this, and the huge mountain of input chips will show them the way. Also, maybe the high Rulers will get to hire more Minions and surrounding players, especially review Rulers, which helps bring more management Rulers and higher pay grades for them as well, to ensure success.

The awkward silence passes and the DoD player starts to get up, bumps the table, and it's an avalanche, it crashes all over the room, scattering into a huge, chaotic mess. He at least seems to recognize the chilling Omen; that it may symbolize what the mountains of growing complex regulations always become. A sick expression appears on his face, involuntarily, just for a moment if you were watching closely.

Out in the hall there's a horrifying, loud piercing screech sound at almost the exact same time, startling the players even more. It's only a janitor's cart in need of maintenance. Still, the players are visibly shaken, one almost faints from its alarming, shocking effect, and they all want to believe it was just a coincidence...

Chapter 3
The Trilogy of Failure

"There's more to leading than proud, clueless following..."

Happy Hour Assembly of the Minions, Circa 2017

"We're leaderless!" my friend Erika exclaimed, *"Just utterly, unequivocally, horribly, fucking leaderless!!"* She had a way with words I liked, and was a genuine person who cared and tried to do the right thing. Club Fed could be really, really tough on this type of person.

She was not furious like some teammates reacted to the Club's madness at times; it was more a sense of true, heart wrenching despair. Something she had put an immense amount of time and effort into was immediately discarded by our Rulers like a frat boy's spent condom. It was the exceptionally rare project that could actually help the Minions, but needed the Rulers to definitely stand up for it to happen since it'd have to go so high up. Thus it had no chance in our scene.

I therefore was more worried than usual in these conversations. I didn't want her to bail, I needed all the sane fellow Minions I could get and I liked her too. I don't recall what I first said, I know I tried to be supportive. I think it was trying to be funny as usual, but more gently, like *"We sure do have a lot of managers but it sure is tough to find a single fucking leader..."*

Which brings us to The Trilogy of Failure.

The Trilogy focuses on three key factors that determine just how much it will suck in a given office, since they determined if the boss sucks or not. But the impact of the Trilogy goes much further since in the Club, most anyone can be your boss. *"Who's not my Boss?"* was a familiar refrain amongst the Minions, a play on the old family comedy show *"Who's the Boss?"*

The iconic movie *"Office Space"* about life in a hopeless bureaucracy was outstanding, it resonated throughout the Federal Government and beyond. But it was the minor leagues, the JV Team, compared to the Club. Its famous line about having eight bosses had to bring a grin (or grimace) to millions in the public sector, at least the working level Minions in huge bureaucracies, since many of us have dozens of bosses or more.

You worked for every layer above you, and there were lots of layers, but also every layer of every surrounding lane that had some part in the process, and the process had lots of parts. We were all in on groupthink and consensus of course, though this was mainly to help spread the wealth, the make-work everyone needed, so they could exist too. It went throughout and way past my activity, involved other DoD branches and agencies we served, yet another DoD lane to pay contractors, and outside of DoD frequently. Such as the U.S. Small Business Administration and occasionally other Club components like the U.S. Government Accountability Office, the General Services Administration, or U.S. Department of Labor, so they could cash in too.

If you produced the paperwork they all needed, grab your ankles, bite the pillow, you know the popular take the pain lines. *"Shut up and take the pain!"* as Tom Berenger's brutal character told the suffering wounded private in the movie *"Platoon."*

Sorry I digressed again there. In any case, there are three key deciding variables, critical pivot points, that make or break a group's leadership and therefore the whole team. If they all go the wrong way you're in big trouble, in Club Fed it's a giant river of smelly excrement, not just a creek. The good news is you could do okay with two of them in your favor, it wouldn't be that bad. Not great, but not unbearable either. In the Club though, all three did go wrong pretty often.

The Three Points of the Triangle

The three points are at least some intelligence or not, some humility or not, and if they really have some authority or not. Let me explain the theory further, showing why only all three aspects going wrong leave you truly screwed. Consider two of three being okay and see where you're at.

Take the terribly arrogant, yet reasonably smart manager who also has some power in a given scene at the Club. This person can be a real condescending jerk, not fun to work for, but when they are smart enough, have some decent knowledge and recognize who else has that or even more, and who can apply it, this was the type of boss I'd get along with just fine. I had this type a good while more than once, and found them to be okay despite their obnoxious, patronizing ways.

Some others didn't like the situation much, even hated it, and I'd ask them *"What if that Ruler was an idiot too, would that go better with their proud micromanagement?"* The bar was pretty low, as mentioned when all three points of the triangle went wrong, it was really bad. *"Lower your expectations and you won't be disappointed,"* was a line I heard early on, which I soon understood well.

Now take the pretty stupid, or let me say innocently clueless manager, and they actually do have some authority in your scene. But if they are reasonably humble too, a decent person, they may even realize to some degree that they don't know much of anything, and defer to people at least their primal instincts tell them are smarter than they are. With just these two, not completely arrogant and with some power in your office, you can be better than okay, more than tolerable. This situation can be darn good really, second only to all three deciding factors on the plus side – intelligent, humble and in power.

That's almost a Club Fed Christmas miracle though, us Minions experienced it very rarely across many dozens of Rulers over the years, more like hundreds considering all the surrounding lanes we answered to. Not unheard of though. It reminded me of rare, way cool wildlife sightings on camping vacations as a kid; lots of cars would pull over to marvel at a magnificent bear prowling a roadside meadow, my brothers and I climbing all over each other to see out of the backseat window, full of awe and wonderment.

Now consider the proud fool that's in supervision but still didn't have any real authority. Plenty of us, especially us persuasive types, could work around them, usually by taking advantage of just how oblivious they were. They didn't notice we were calling the shots for them, like getting them to believe they came up with the pathway we'd just clued them in on. We could especially work around them if there was someone strong and controlling enough, and not too dumb, above them, which was usually what left them powerless.

It didn't need to be immediately above them, there were so many layers that if just one wasn't too bad up from them, you could deal with your proud, clueless direct Ruler. Looking back at it, I guess there was some skill development from this, managing upward trying not to upset the arrogant, inept and impotent boss by learning to be more manipulative.

Cowardice was usually there despite the pride, it helped since even when they were outwardly very confident, it was *cowardice masquerading as bravado.* You could still leverage that fear to get a little something sort of done, like that higher up who carried some weight being really pissed if at least a tiny sign of progress wasn't there. Or a powerful reviewer, someone in legal they were scared of awaiting their turn to review, which I'm sorry to say was about everyone in legal. I did like the many attorneys I dealt with at the Club over the years, but there were maybe two out of dozens I'd hire voluntarily, as we already touched on in the last chapter.

In fact some Homies and I originally coined *"There's more to leading than scared following..."* when it came to the fear factor that was such a powerful influence at the Club. I used the line at the start of this chapter instead, but it's a very close call.

All in all, I'd say the proud, pretty clueless if not plain stupid, but thankfully powerless boss or immediate Ruler, was probably the most common type in my years at the Club. Let me share an example which may sum that up pretty well...

Yosemite – A Profile in Proud Impotence

Yosemite got his nickname by reminding us of the old *"Yosemite Sam"* cartoons, with that funny, short Wild West type character yelling *"What in tarnation?!"* as he furiously shot off his cowboy revolvers. Yosemite was an excitable, short guy with a temper, he'd sputter and stammer when worked up, we truly could not decipher what the hell he was trying to say much of the time. He was a classic been-there-done-that guy too, though no one had seen him do anything in his many years at the Club.

He was good at talking about himself in the third person, and when he'd boldly proclaim *"Nobody tells Yosemite how to run his office!"* it was a sure sign he'd cave like a house of cards as soon as anyone above him saw things differently. Incidentally, that quote was only lucid because I had learned to listen closely to his bumbling gibberish and translate it for my fellow Minions.

When he was my boss I still liked him well enough, definitely entertaining, and we'd of course stroke his ego, laugh at his dumb jokes, you know the drill. Go along to get along. While making a really good Ruler salary he'd buy his suits from Goodwill, and would somehow seem to find what got donated there from boxes of outfits last seen at 1980s garage sales around Las Vegas. Wild, flamboyant colors and patterns, shiny, with super wide lapels, you'd think he was auditioning for some sort of old swingers movie filmed in the Sin City. Just oblivious.

Incidentally though, I can't knock one saving their hard-earned Club bucks on the wardrobe. I had a favorite pair of khaki's last probably 10 years, wearing them about twice a week, not washing them much to help them last. But they still were super well-made and durable, plus I also liked them since their cut and build made me look like I was a part-time porn star, especially while sitting down. I still wear them to church on occasion.

Anyway, while Yosemite was my boss we had gained a new review Ruler in our policy office, she was attractive and very arrogant, therefore irresistible to Yosemite and another clownish Ruler who were both constantly trying to hit on her. You know, the usual male mating instinct kicking in despite no chance in hell, the pursuer looking completely ridiculous. Okay yes I was not immune to that in my day, but I do believe I figured out a few life lessons by the time I was 40 or so.

I sure didn't like this new review Ruler, she was giving us Minions lots of shit at every turn, all sorts of perceived findings in our make-work, which of course were guaranteed by our broken methods. She had no understanding of that, however, since like many in her shoes she had no experience whatsoever doing make-work as a Minion.

Well one day that had really added up, I had yet another long laundry list of alleged blunders to deal with, and I ended up asking her just what the hell qualified her as an expert in what she's never done. Spoiled Princess that she was, we dumb males kissing her ass her whole life, that was very upsetting, and she formally filed a complaint against me.

It was Yosemite's turn to shine, could this be the ticket to finally get in her tight pant suit? Never mind that he and I had got along without issue for years. As my boss he'd put me in my place and win over Hell's Princess.

He called me into his office, presenting me the first of just two formal reprimand attempts I ever faced in my entire career. Otherwise I was not a trouble maker, not that they knew of. But this was too much, I'd learned to take a lot from proud fools in my day but I just couldn't this time.

I started with a grim, leaning-in, not too loud *"Are...you...fucking... kidding...me?"* with the pauses for effect, and went on to dress him down pretty good I thought. Not in a rage at all like he would, just with a direct, firm resolve, conveying a sense of on-the-brink of absolute fury that wouldn't go well for him, at least it seemed he saw it that way.

Now I'm not saying I'm a rock by any means, I was nervous too, basically always one to avoid confrontation. But anyone with a spine at all has their limits, just isn't going to take it at some point.

He was speechless, trembling, completely aghast that this usually mild-mannered, subservient Minion was letting him have it. I pointed out all the overtime fraud, time cheating, absolutely egregious performance failures, assorted office tantrums, just a shitload of wrongs that never even faced the slightest of consequences in our scene, while not naming anyone, of course. Yet I get a reprimand for a single true statement a complete bitch he wants to bang didn't like.

To his credit, he tore up the reprimand and we never had another problem at all.

The point of this example is just that he, and others like him, were I'm sorry to say ultimately scared and weak, the dumb bravado a cover, though I'd imagine plenty of readers know this well too. I just offer it as the embodiment of this type of Ruler in the Trilogy, and this type was common at the Club.

To conclude this chapter let me just say that when it comes to the Trilogy, you're only truly screwed if all points of the triangle go the wrong way. If you did find yourself in the Bermuda Triangle of Club Fed, and thinking that completely disappearing from the face of the earth without a trace would be better than years trying to put up with a dumb, proud boss who also has authority in your scene, you can still find a way. This will be covered more in the Assimilation chapter. It's still all good ultimately, it really is. *So shut up and take the pain!*

Chapter 4
Self-Awareness Deficit Disorder (SADD)

"You can't fix stupid."

From legendary Comedian Ron White, 2006

"Do you know who you're talking to?!" the High Ruler demanded, barely able to control their rage at the sheer audacity of the Minion who didn't seem to recognize their status. *"Need I remind you that I'm the Deputy Assistant Undersecretary to the Director of the United States Department of Defense's Department of Redundancy Department?!!"*

The Ruler was beyond dismayed at the Minion's apparent disrespect. They'd worked hard for many years to get where they were at, starting as just another Minion themselves long ago. But their sheer talent, their abilities and just plain hard work, brought them higher and higher at the Club.

They rose to greatness, and it had been more than earned. In their mind they had accomplished more than anyone, maybe the most grandiose reports ever issued about nothing, or they developed new policies never before needed that became essential. They then led increasing number of Minions along the way, the paperwork quality from those offices second to none in their field. They had accomplished all sorts of feats within Club Fed that few, if any, had matched.

That really was not much of an exaggeration when it came to the worst cases of this phenomenon at the Club, a condition we eventually called SADD – Self-Awareness Deficit Disorder.

SADD Definition, Signs, Symptoms

Self-Awareness Deficit Disorder is marked by an ongoing pattern of self-important behaviors that interfere with functioning or development. People with SADD may have difficulty understanding they have any weaknesses, and tend to believe they only have strengths. They consistently perceive others to be inferior, and can believe they are omnipotent, including being highly gifted in their field as well as all other aspects of their existence. SADD sufferers also tend to be delusional, imagining they are highly accomplished when they display no evidence of any meaningful accomplishment. They have difficulty with contextual thinking, including a tendency to be distracted by, or focused on, the irrelevant while not being able to understand what may be important to a given situation.

It was not difficult to diagnose SADD, the signs and symptoms were obvious. You'd deal with it in an example like the one above, there were so many players that you'd get slapped in the face for your insolence at the get-go, in a first encounter if you didn't see it coming, hadn't got a scouting report or other warning.

You'd find out quickly then - how they carried themselves of course; their attitude toward lesser beings, the very proud demeanor, the condescending smiles when in a good mood, the looks of disapproval or even a simmering, glaring anger when displeased. Sometimes the SADD sufferers even spoke of themselves in the third person, like Yosemite in the last chapter.

The impressive position titles and certifications were usually a definite sign, often in their emails. Not always, some who showed that SADD symptom still turned out to be okay. But it told you to proceed with caution until you knew. Yeah I know, this happens most everywhere. But I bet it doesn't match the Club's versions. Remember, many if not most of the alleged positions don't even exist outside of the government. That's a major distinction, someone could rise to the top in a basically fake job or organization, and easily see it as the equivalent of being CEO of a Fortune 500 Company. They genuinely believed it, though many of the rest of us, I believe most, knew they were delusional, suffering from a severe case of SADD.

It wasn't just the Rulers, plenty of the people in roles surrounding the Minions, since they signed or reviewed our make-work, or even in gigs which in theory were to support us, suffered from SADD. One secretary showed so many titles and certifications below her name in email, a bunch of it in assorted voluntary feel good programs which had impressive titles, that I thought no fucking way could all of it be held by just one person. Maybe she identified as schizophrenic. But one dared not displease her; she was too connected as well. Unassailable, no matter how she conducted herself.

One day she blurted out in a large team building class, getting fed up with a few impudent Minions suggesting they should be allowed to decide the content of a sentence, that we all worked for her and must do as we're told, by our office's lead secretary (if you could pick that out of the 13 titles in her signature block). She meant it, and the highest Ruler of our office was there and didn't say a word.

I was scolded by her for my incompetence many times, most everyone was. What was great though, and us Minions would share these with each other for laughs, is when she used email to admonish us, which was most of these occasions, she could rarely write a single coherent sentence. Our area's highest ranking secretary was illiterate.

I know much of this gets pretty harsh. Don't get me wrong, there really are some capable, talented, even relatively accomplished people in Fed leadership and other roles, I did encounter some who were impressive. Not surprisingly though, they had at least some humility, if in a Ruler gig they hit the three points in the Trilogy we covered in the last chapter.

They had some self-awareness, like most of us, realizing we don't know everything, subscribing to the famously true *"The more you learn, the more you realize how little you know."* Even when you've learned a hell of a lot about a given topic, healthy minded people realize there are always others who know more. Strengths and weaknesses, hopefully most people are at least somewhat aware of theirs, and also think of the context surrounding what they believe they have accomplished. Is it all really that amazing, did you discover a brand new, way better form of clean energy, or maybe a vaccine for COVID that actually prevents it? Or maybe you ruled teams that brought more office policies achieving nothing, truly an amazing, historic feat which surpasses those examples.

The good Rulers and other solid people we had were often still in arguably pretend roles, but you'd find ability, and what was funny is some of them, even a few High Rulers, when they recognized you saw things like they did, would sometimes reveal it, often in a covert way. I enjoyed those moments, a knowing look, almost a wink, occasionally even a quiet joke about white collar welfare.

However too many people, and I'd bet any day more than even the most messed up private sector scenes, truly had no signs of self-awareness at all. They had little or no identifiable ability, no meaningful accomplishments, and still really did great for themselves, partly due to all the questionable but celebrated roles, but also all the people in the Club like them that not only didn't recognize a fellow fuck-up, they valued it and often promoted it. *"Fuck up move up"* was a popular line many active duty military and veterans told me while working at the Club.

The worst SADD cases were consistently inept, disorganized, lacking people skills, often dishonest, afraid to make any decision, all in all the least capable people you'd know. Their single identifiable ability seemed to be tossing up word salads that didn't make a single legit point. Yet in some ways you could understand why they thought they were amazing. They had reached a very prestigious position, at least they believed it was. They were usually very highly educated, though not in anything useful it seemed like, no true demonstrated ability to get something done. But obviously they brought the most talent, wisdom, ability and accomplishment to the Club.

Those suffering the most from SADD had usually done the least in terms of anything resembling a deliverable along the way, like the make-work of the Minions. If they had been Minions, they had done the least in those roles, but sincerely believed they did the most. They often disappeared when something finally had to get done somehow, making it look good like an illness or fake class they had to complete on time, and other Minions took care of their make-work.

That was one of the early warning signs of SADD. Or a good sign for them in that if it was deemed wrong, it was on the other Minions stepping in. But if it became a perceived success it was still their assignment, they delivered the win. Some would also realize they could participate in developing another new input like we covered in the Outputs are Inputs chapter, and position themselves for advancement.

Yes, yes we all know it's about playing the game wherever you go. At least political skill: stroking the right people, especially being associated with happenings along the way which are believed to be successful. So I will acknowledge many SADD cases at least displayed that. You didn't execute anything really, but were seen as involved in some way like an input project, in an oversight capacity, or ruling something, though always with other Rulers.

So when things went wrong, the surrounding and Ruling roles were so diluted at the Club that its worst clowns never did anything wrong either. Just the Minions or maybe sometimes others already going nowhere were blamed. The opposite of most real world scenarios, where the first one to go when things go very badly, is the General Manager or the Head Coach, for example, or the department head at the private sector business gets canned because their section is failing, which is their responsibility.

Maybe the most incredible example of how things worked at the Club in terms of Rulers suffering from SADD not recognizing it in other Rulers, and no actual accountability in any way, was a lasting blunder that finally was clearly found to waste tens of millions of dollars for many years. It truly was a serious crime. I'm not talking about the processes on this one, those wasted countless millions every year, billions collectively across DoD. That was normal, no worries at all, almost no one grasped the regular institutionalized DoD and Federal level waste in our practices.

This was different, a clear and obvious fuck up no one picked up on before, easily corrected if the Rulers in the office had even the slightest clue about anything, paid just a bit of attention. When it finally was corrected, the Rulers in charge of the area responsible faced no consequences for the fortunes lost for many years on their watch, clearly under their responsibility.

They weren't far removed from it either, which would be a mitigating factor one could agree. However, this was not a big office by Club standards. Nope, these Rulers instead got major awards with high level agency acclaim, for saving millions for DoD and the taxpayer from that day forward. For rescuing you from them, you could say. One of them later got a big promotion.

Also remember that in the Club, the underlying premise is all methods and processes required by the Rulers are completely sound, so it was easy to see who really messed up something, never a Ruler or other surrounding gig. Maybe that was a factor in the travesty I just covered, the higher Rulers knew that the two Rulers involved couldn't possibly have fucked it up, no matter what. Only the Minions could lose millions, though I think it was so obvious on that one that they at least couldn't bring themselves to punish any Minions. But bad news was still on someone else, even if not named. All good news was because of you, or you were at least seen as a main contributor to the success. One has to acknowledge there's at least some learned or natural ability to being good at that.

Yes that really does happen everywhere to different degrees it seems. However, and it is admittedly limited, but my experience outside the Club, and as a constantly intrigued and even amazed observer of such things in general, suggests no one can top the Club when it comes to ridiculous people that could still do great, even rise to the top.

One of the many benefits to my particular job is I dealt with successful businesses a lot, including many close dealings through all sorts of bureaucratic shit shows we threw at them. There was no comparison, almost universally their capabilities showed; in fact it was very refreshing after many of my dealings that were strictly within the Club. I'm not saying all were completely honest people, you still needed to pay attention, not be a trusting fool. But these folks could find and execute real solutions, which were needed for all the roadblocks, even if manufactured by a messed up Club establishment.

Often I dealt with the founding entrepreneur directly given the amount of money involved, the company presidents, and was consistently impressed, one could clearly see why they were successful, including that they had always got something done to get paid. In Club Fed we may well have to fire someone like that, we'd look just too absurd in comparison.

Then again I guess we wouldn't look that silly, because too many were oblivious to what real ability and demonstrated accomplishment were, versus imagined. Let me share maybe the most fascinating case of SADD I ever dealt with, though a lot competed for the title:

A SADD Case Study: Enter the Dragon Lady

Credit goes to the iconic Bruce Lee movie *"Enter the Dragon"* for that subtitle, it seemed to fit here. The Dragon Lady looked, and really was, terrifying. I first met her when I was on a trip to a distant office that was part of our Club, and I'll never forget it. I thought she wasn't our employee at first, maybe she was visiting from a movie set nearby, playing the offspring of Godzilla or a Velociraptor.

She was big, angry, with a mean, almost demonic looking face, but you couldn't see it well she wore so much make-up, as much as multiple circus clowns at once, but in sort of a sick caricature of an ugly Cleopatra rendition. Certainly anything but pretty, though she nailed the very dark and deep set eyes in an effective, very scary way. Menacing.

That gave one pause by itself, but she wore revealing clothes too, at least around her huge chest, and it looked like her flesh may have actually been decaying in front of your eyes. Like a zombie, maybe from the *"Walking Dead"* series, she might not even be a living, breathing human. The Dragon Lady's provocative zombie clothes looked like recycled drapes from an old, real trashy mobile home too.

Then I got scared, seriously rattled, a different kind of shock than you'll read about in the next chapter. It dawned on me that she could have been resurrected from the long ago dead, an unwrapped mummification of an infamously cruel tyrant of centuries past, ruling some ancient empire with absolute brutality. No wonder why she was so pissed all the time as I quickly found out. Her gig now had to really suck compared to the one she had in 1,400 BC, flogging or beheading anyone who didn't bow to her power and greatness.

She sure let me know immediately that she was amazing, clearly she knew more than everyone, every topic; you name it she was an expert. She had of course done more than everyone in our Club too, an extreme case of the been-there-done-that thing. She insisted she had trained me somewhere before, though I sure hadn't ever met her. No fucking way anyone could forget or even just *"unsee"* The Dragon, another sign of her being delusional. Everyone else in our realm was an amateur at best, or more likely a bumbling inept clown compared to her. She sure was no clown. She just looked like one - a zombie, mummy clown.

She even believed she had once dated an accomplished NFL player then dumped him for being such a loser, maybe since he didn't make the Pro Bowl. Seriously, Dragon Lady? A blind, deaf and dumb NFL player? That redefined surreal in my book.

Luckily my assignment on the trip was fully pretend; I was to review her work and others. Fittingly for such assignments in the Club, I didn't know much about what they allegedly did in her office. I had signed up for the assignment as a break from my usual Minion status, but also since I wanted to visit the really nice area there, my usual reason for the occasional trip I took. I enjoyed seeing more of America that way, the taxpayer funding my travel costs, and I often added some vacation days to check things out.

Needless to say I gave her glowing reviews, in part since I didn't know differently, but mainly because I was afraid to death not to. But even not knowing much about her make-work, I could tell she was completely incompetent. Her desk a total mess, you couldn't even find it under the heaps of files and scattered paperwork, but more significantly her documents made no sense at all, by any standard, and you couldn't find lots of what was rumored to be there. Incoherent entries and writings, content from actions unrelated to what the document was to address, furious scribbling at times, just ridiculous.

The Dragon Lady was lucky to have a job at all, anywhere, but I wasn't surprised that she was highly regarded by the Rulers of our Club. I think mainly it was they were just too afraid not to praise and promote her. Then a few years later the most terrifying news I ever got at the Club had arrived...

The Dragon Lady became my boss, my immediate Ruler.

Well you have to find the positives no matter what happens along the way; that much we should all learn. No way could I ever imagine a worse boss from hell, even the worst of those before and after her were angels sent straight from heaven. Us Minions were abused every day, especially considering the usual cushy, even coddled ways we were used to at the Club.

However she'd be horrific anywhere, psychological warfare constantly, angry outburst including temper tantrums, furious blaming, written reprimands on us for what she had actually done, like losing our shit from a file then writing us up for it not being there. No one cheated on their time more than the chain smoking, fire-breathing Dragon, though she punished Minions for small time infractions.

You'd hear her slamming stuff around in her office after scolding us, or from emails that upset her; then she'd storm out to chain smoke. Thank God someone had invented smoking. She made me absolutely want to hug and kiss the Marlboro Man if it was him. We'd get good long breaks from the cruel tyranny several times a day, taking deep breaths for a while but always the sense of dread while awaiting her return.

We thought of group suicide. We could make Club Fed history, defy the Dragon Lady, defy the evil Rulers that sentenced us to her, maybe we'd all jump together off the roof of the tall building we worked in, screaming *"Freedom!!"* as our final act of public service, then live on in infamy. *"Fuck you Dragon Lady and Rulers, who's going to do your make-work now?!"*

Okay that was just in jest at Minion drinking outings, but I think a couple of us did consider it and several really started drinking a lot, maybe fantasizing about a drunk driving prison term to get away from her a good while. We knew we wouldn't be fired for that at least.

One Minion, it was Dante actually, one of my best buddies, was definitely no joke, a very strong, capable guy. Division I college athletes like Dante take plenty of pain, all sorts of injuries and setbacks, they know how to work through adversity and Dante even got his degree in a serious major too. But he did have very high blood pressure, and it just got higher. It would soar in encounters with the Dragon Lady, especially her fits, and we worried about him. Dante was our Rocky, and the Dragon Lady might break him.

Well this SADD Case Study could go on, so much more I could share. But alas, even in the total dysfunction and cowardice of the Club this had to end at some point. Something had to be done, so many complaints to higher Rulers, plus many formal grievances to the Equal Employment Opportunity Office and local Federal Employee Union, the Rulers just hated those. I didn't file any of them but I did encourage others too. Cowardly of me I know, sparing myself her worst wrath. Their choice though, and I sure didn't complain.

Then one day it finally ended, and before the long, slow grind to address the nightmare, such as finding a place to move her where she may somehow be less of a catastrophe. Again, remember no one gets fired at the Club. But a true miracle had occurred; I knew then that God was indeed real...

The Dragon Lady got promoted to a higher Ruler gig in a different Club scene.

We prayed for their souls that day, as we raised our glasses high.

Ever since the phenomenon of SADD was first discovered and carefully researched by us Minions in constant clinical studies and trials at the Club, I kept seeing it all over, especially on the news. A SADD Pandemic it seemed like, a Pomposity Pandemic if you will, just totally out of control narcissism. Mostly I saw it clearly showing in high ranking politicians of both major parties, a SADD Trickle Down effect possibly then afflicting our Rulers at the Club. But also elite media people and celebrities bloviating with complete confidence about what they seemed to have absolutely no clue on.

However in those examples, the SADD sufferers had achieved way more, at least for themselves, than our Rulers. I'm not saying the highest profile Government SADD cases accomplished anything for their country, unless you count helping to make all our lives poorer and more dangerous. I'm just saying they managed to do way better for themselves than for example, the Deputy Assistant of Such and Such example at the start of this chapter. I'm not excusing it in anyone, either. Don't me wrong, I'm just saying I can understand why it happens in some cases more than others.

Well there's just one more sad part to this chapter on SADD, and here it is...

<u>SADD Treatments:</u>

(This space intentionally left blank. There are no known treatments for SADD.)

Chapter 5
The Four Stages of Assimilation

Detective Rust Cohie, played by Matthew McConaughey in the "True Detective" Series, as told to a murder suspect facing impending doom as the overwhelming evidence closed in on her...

"I gotta' get the hell outta' here," my newer buddy Roberto was really pissed, *"These people are fucking nuts, truly delusional!"* I responded only with my best looks of concern, understanding and sympathy, anticipating he wanted to vent more before I said anything.

I'd had this exchange many times in my day. When they weren't too upset I'd reply with *"Welcome to our shit show, Homie!"* or some other smart ass comment. But when they were clearly distraught or furious, it was best just to listen at first, letting them have at it.

"These assholes demand that I get this done, but they find every reason to not let me get it done!" Roberto went on to share more of the sad story, though I could practically tell him the tale before he told me, I'd experienced it so many times and observed it with others. What he had to get done was extremely unlikely to resemble anything the military needed, in this case an elaborate high visibility report of some sort, but it was believed to be urgently needed. Meanwhile Rulers and other players involved were afraid to support it in case

the review and audit armies, or higher Rulers, found it to be wrong, which they usually did, especially this high level of an exercise. So every objection or *"concern"* imaginable was thrown at the poor fucker.

He went on with it a while, he was on Revision 14 of the report by then, tears almost welling up in his eyes at times. When he seemed ready, it was time for me once again to explain the Four Stages of Federal Employee Assimilation...

<u>Stage 1 - Shock and Awe</u>

This stage was named after a phrase I originally learned of in the first Iraq War when the U.S. Military hit Iraqi forces so hard and overwhelmingly they were quickly rendered helpless, desperate and essentially already defeated. They immediately understood resistance would prove to be futile.

The impact of this stage on a newer federal employee, depending on their specific circumstances of course, can be frighteningly similar. *Just absolutely blown away by how much complex mind-numbing dysfunctional procedure can be manufactured, and how much scrutiny and often urgent pressure can be created, to get a little something done occasionally, even if it didn't matter at all toward any identifiable result.*

When this first hits the newer employee, it hits them hard. It's upsetting. They can believe they suddenly found themselves in a scary revolving door and can't get out.

One analogy I can offer is it's like you are chest deep trying to fight your way upstream in a raging flood, with all sorts of obstacles hitting you - floating tree branches, assorted garbage, tumbling furniture and household appliances... You look over to the shore and dozens of people are there studying you very closely under some shade trees, critiquing and scoring your every move, none of them lifting a finger to help you.

Plus a few dozen more of them are upstream chucking a bunch more shit into the floodwaters.

As mentioned though, the specific job or fake job in question, and surrounding circumstances, mean everything as to how bad this stage is, or even if you experienced it at all. Most do to some degree at least. It's hardest on those positions that have to produce the documentation deliverables all the other jobs need to justify themselves, and toughest of all on those who took the red pill and realize that.

If they took the blue pill path of ignorance, believing everything manufactured to do is real and necessary, it was usually not as bad in my experience. I believe it was probably not as infuriating since they never realized that so many in their environment, especially most of the Rulers, won't ever understand that their own remarkably dysfunctional methods are the entire reason for the shock and awe inspiring madness.

What's funny is it can still hit even those that don't have to produce the documents cooked up as allegedly needed for something to happen. Even the surrounding roles, like compiling surrounding elaborate reports on the manufactured documents, as was the case with Roberto's task that time, could face this phenomenon.

I'd let them know, very gently if needed, or more often with my best efforts to use humor, that they will be okay. What they are experiencing happens to everyone, and it will pass. But not before it gets worse...

<u>Stage 2 – Anger</u>

Let's say you entered the Club at a relatively young age like I did, also with a positive attitude about what you'd be doing like supporting our nation's military, your work therefore purposeful, the start of a rewarding and fulfilling career. Or maybe you were in another career type job, possibly even another in a government gig or related to it, and you had your reasons for taking this one, believing it would somehow be better. Okay probably mainly the pay or location but also likely still seeking a sense of contribution or accomplishment, which I'd say most people agree is what brings job satisfaction.

Then it hits you. Right in the chops. A Mike Tyson knockout punch of shock and awe like we just covered. *Just. Fucking. Brutal.*

So then comes the anger. *What the hell have I just done?! Now all I can think of is getting the fuck out of here. But it sure was an undertaking to get this gig in the first place, and I moved halfway across the country too, for hell's sake! What am I doing with my life, just what the fuck do I do now?! This is beyond awful. Where did I put my meds?! Where in God's name is the nearest fucking liquor store?!!*

There were often clear signs of panic with the anger from people in this stage, maybe too shocked in the first stage to feel panic, more of an awed numbness, a genuine sense of deep disbelief and denial at first, back in Stage 1.

This Stage 2 was the hardest phase for newer people. But it got easier for almost everyone from here, it really did. Teammates who had been through it were helpful for the most part. Most were decent people, even the dim-witted ones. And if they didn't care much they could definitely relate, and would still be good to talk to. I always welcomed the counseling opportunities, somehow it helped me when I tried to help them, at a minimum letting them know they are not alone. For me it wasn't some noble sense of caring really, just revisiting this for some laughs and to help me not fall back into it.

Plus I had another motive – if I was working with them, discovered they were not an idiot and I actually liked them, which was a lot of the time I'm happy to say, I wanted them to get past this. I wanted them to stay to make my life easier. I watched too many good ones leave, the sheer madness was just too much, a number of them I thought were our smartest, which then seemed to bring them the most pain since they quickly saw everything for what it was. We did lose Roberto and Jackie this way, and many more. Then when we did get a proud clown on board instead, another future SADD case, my gig suffered. I was often their trainer or had to sign their stupid shit at least, then take the establishment's shit for it.

However, the main factor in getting past this stage, or any other tough times really, is of course attitude. I had to work on that a lot, still too often didn't succeed, but emphasizing all the great aspects of life in Club Fed truly did always outweigh the suck. So that is what I focused on both in my own assimilation, and when I tried to help others. The angry phase varied a lot in duration, and yes myself and others would unfortunately digress at times, as mentioned some really good people never did get past it and left. But eventually most people would reach the next phase...

<u>Stage 3 - Acceptance</u>

It might initially feel like defeat, selling out your soul to the establishment, the Matrix if you will. But accepting your fate in the hopeless bureaucracies of Club Fed, and that resistance is futile, can instead be cleansing, liberating, a truly freeing sense of release. It's a big win if you let it be that. It's not giving in and taking the blue pill of ignorance, you still know it's mostly fake. You're not in denial of the gargantuan train wreck you spend over 2,000 precious waking hours a year of your life in. You're making the best of it, focusing on all the benefits, all that really does outweigh the suck.

Embrace it, you can do this! That's what I'd tell people, and it took a while but eventually I really did mean it. Of course no one could blame the very smart people that decided to bail, they were definitely marketable too, readily hired for more real jobs. So this strictly applied to those that stuck it out. You'd better find a way to accept your fate or else your life would be miserable, or worse.

There absolutely are so many good aspects of life in Club Fed. Generous steady pay, benefits including ample time off and flexible work hours, incredible job security... I've found credible evidence including on cbo.gov (https://www.cbo.gov/publication/52637) showing that Feds are paid significantly more in total pay and benefits for equivalent positions than in the private sector, other than those with Professional or Doctorate degrees. I don't doubt that including my experience with plenty of friends and contacts outside of Club Fed. But I do wonder how many pay comparisons can be made with lots of positions that don't exist at all outside of the Club.

You have to really, really try hard if you wanted to get fired. I bet you could drop a big Cleveland Steamer, you know the biggest wet dump of your life, on a high ranking Ruler's desk and at most maybe get some time off (with pay). I read that a federal employee is 45 times less likely to be fired than a private sector counterpart (thehill.com, 4/14/2019). To me it seemed more like at least 400 times less likely. I think I saw it twice in 33 years and those two nut jobs very scary, possible homicidal maniacs. It turned out I did work alongside a convicted pedophile for years, though none of us knew that until after he retired. Maybe they were already calling it Minor Attracted Person, before the rest of us heard of that new way cool term, so they deemed it okay.

Plus the Club really is crazy funny too, constant entertainment if you keep the right perspective. Some of us Minions would get together and celebrate all the comedic moments that would compete for the best feats of the week, or whatever timeframe. I'd get pissed when I missed a really good one, like the ancient, angry Fossil marching into our highest Ruler's office early one morning demanding that he fire himself for his incompetence since he didn't declare that day a snow day - early enough so The Fossil could know before his chosen 5:00 am start time.

There were so, so many funny experiences. Another classic I did get to see was Letch using an email to apologize to a large group of contractors, with a big part of our Club scene cc'd including many High Rulers, on behalf of the entire United States Government. I loved that one, except for maybe some of my Rulers thinking I goaded him into it. I didn't, not that one anyway.

Then again there were a few funny memories I'd still rather *"unsee."* The huge old office building I spent most of my career in featured lots of empty rooms and halls not being used. One time I was entering a favorite forgotten conference room to take a power nap and a stampede of large mammals seemed to break loose. I got a glimpse of at least three sets of big bare butt cheeks scrambling for cover in the half-darkness before I shut the door. Maybe they were filming *"The 50 Shades of Club Fed."* Who knows, but the Club scene was legendary for certain extra *Federal Affairs* getting busted at times. Maybe lots of Feds with lots of time on their hands made it inevitable.

Anyway, with a good attitude life in Club Fed is beyond good, which brings me to the next and final phase...

<u>Stage 4 – Celebration</u>

Not everyone gets here, which is okay since Acceptance is still very good. But I believe myself and other friends of mine like Dante, and my boss Sam, even reached Stage 4, Celebration. It didn't always last; you might fall back into just Acceptance, even occasionally Anger a bit, all the way back to Stage 2, regrettably. But never Stage 1, Shock and Awe, absolutely nothing could shock you when you'd been at this long enough. You've seen it all, or at least so much that even the most totally absurd, beyond ridiculous events or new, remarkably dysfunctional processes, wouldn't surprise you at all.

It's sick and twisted, *but you actually enjoyed it the more totally insane it got.*

I know this sounds even more jaded, but it's not. We learned to just love it most of the time. An important part of our thinking, and I mean this seriously, is a shift away from seeing your gig in the Club as needing to bring you any job satisfaction at all. We realized it's a truly great means, an arguably unbeatable roadmap to plenty of satisfaction and fulfillment in the rest of your life.

Doing right by your family hopefully first and foremost, setting all sorts of goals let's say in your favorite pastimes and interests, whatever causes you care about, working hard to reach those goals and attaining them. The Club Fed lifestyle not only allows the financial means, but its schedule flexibility, time off and other advantages probably are among the best gigs for supporting other life goals. We did have one of our best people that left, and was very successful in the private sector for years, return to the Club because the work/life balance was so much better. Katrina made a good call on that, I thought.

Some of the most capable and ambitious in the Club ran their own businesses from their desks, or these days from home if working remotely. The steady Fed income and scheduling flexibility helped provide their ventures significant advantages compared to people completely on their own, trying to be fully self-employed. Plenty had so little to do much of the time, even despite the manufactured processes, that their second job was their primary job, but on the Fed clock. I knew people with dozens of rental properties that kept them busy, lawn care services, snowplowing, tax accounting, it was a long list. Also creative writing, someone I know pretty well did that on the Fed clock at times, when caught up on his make-work.

I began to wonder, especially as working remotely became mainstream, if we actually had some people working two full-time Club Fed jobs at once, using a false identify for one of them, so they got two big paydays. They may have even held a Club gig outside of the one with us but which had a related touch, which then had them sign their alias on the same form they had signed and sent from our office. Let's just hope they'd be fucking decent enough to not require too many revisions first.

I tried to become an entrepreneur myself a good while many years back, a little extra income for several years. Not a smart business idea though, printed periodicals facing the inevitable when the web took off. Plus I found myself pretty stuck in the relative production side of the Club, not as much free time while cranking out countless documents for the broad establishment to feast on. Granted part of it was me being too lazy to try hard enough for one of the sweeter surrounding gigs.

There was another reason to celebrate, again this may sound cynical but I sincerely don't mean to be on this note. One would learn to put up with so much astonishing bullshit for anything to get done at all, even in a small pretend way, that when you were on your own pursuing whatever real goals you were after, it was truly, absolutely heaven sent.

The sheer futility of the Club actually motivated us to work harder at reaching goals outside of it.

Sure there will always be lots of setbacks in any worthwhile objective. But when they are way more in your control, entirely in many cases, it's all on you, and more satisfying that way I'd say. When I'd totally mess up one of my big home improvement projects, even after five times the time, effort and cost I expected, it'd still ultimately feel great to correct and finish it myself. Even if it got done with capable help I could arrange, it was so much better than no fix at all that I was allowed to decide.

Lastly on this note, one should consider, at least if they've been in the Club a long time, that in many cases their job skills, if you'd call it that, really aren't marketable outside the Club. Yes I know there are significant exceptions, but lots of us do what doesn't exist outside the Federal Government. I'm sorry, but so much of it really is pretend. So what do you bring to the table, why should a successful growing business hire you? Did you review and sign a form or two a week, checking that a bunch of codes met an irrelevant policy? Are you a skilled Facebook Analyst too? Impressive.

Personally, I didn't develop much ability that anyone else would hire. Plus I'd have trouble succeeding at a demanding Burger King job again, or cleaning filthy truck stop restrooms again (though it was educational for a 15 year old), or working long hours in retail again, as just a few of the shit jobs I think back on. I'd have even way more trouble starting my own business from scratch, and tip my hat to everyone who succeeds at that. Hell yes, give me Club Fed any day.

Chapter 6
Understanding Bureaucracitis

"The fish isn't sick, the water's dirty"

From the book by this title, by Leadership Consultant Steven Gaffney, 2009

"None of us is as dumb as all of us"

Origins unknown, but available evidence suggests they worked at the Club.

Those are such good lines they both seemed to fit here.

As mentioned in the Prologue, I'm trying to present my ramblings in a somewhat organized manner, hopefully getting some legitimate points across too. Now it's time to pull together what we've covered so far. What a typical day, most days, are like at the Club, what people experience there. The Inputs being the Outputs, the Trilogy of Failure, SADD, and their roles in, and effects on, the institution. The Four Stages faced by those in the Club, and its impact on them. We're trying to get at real meaning here. This is serious shit, damn it! So I submit this now all brings us to what we called *"Bureaucracitis"*:

<u>Bureaucracitis definition, signs and symptoms:</u>

Bureaucracitis is a way an individual's mind, or more commonly a large institution's collective thinking and subsequent practices, process information as well as try to function, which then becomes completely dysfunctional. It can cause a loss of touch with reality, replacing it with one or more alternate realities, believing in what is not real, including increasingly complex processes that guarantee failure being perceived as essential to the individual's or institution's success and well-being, so more misguided practices are added which bring even more dysfunction. The ability to reason and apply context is severely impaired, the irrelevant is believed to be critical and vice versa.

It can be triggered by mental illness, such as Self-Awareness Deficit Disorder (SADD), a common individual condition which may contribute to an institution's Bureaucracitis. Such possible factors as trauma from shocking experiences and practices may also contribute, which can lead to anger and confusion, compounding the impacts of the condition. Sheer idiocy is believed to be a contributing factor as well, namely in the collective, not necessarily individual, sense. But more research is needed on possible causes and treatments for Bureaucracitis.

I'll try not to spend too much time discussing Bureaucracitis. It really is a summary of what's been covered, what it all adds up to. As mentioned in The Outputs are Inputs, one of the many remarkable practices we faced, is that a summary of something should greatly exceed the total content and detail of what one is summarizing. Duplicate everything and a bunch of other shit too. We're trying not to be that stupid here. I'm retired now; I don't have to roll that way.

We're after what this all means at this point, the takeaways. Let me offer this...

Bureaucracitis, the extreme bureaucratic condition we faced, prevented the Club from functioning in any effective way. The focus was on process and procedure inputs, most of them manufactured with little or no understanding of real outputs, or a commitment to objectives not related to real results for the military, so those true and necessary results failed, especially in any sense of their remarkable process costs and time to accomplish anything at all. This created a cycle of stupid consisting of more inputs, and our failure to meet them, which was then met by creating even more inputs in response. All thought was focused on following the expanding micro-regulations and procedures due to the extreme micromanagement applied to show the mostly meaningless coverage was met or not, instead of productive, results-first or solution-oriented thinking. The organization, at least the part that tried to do anything, suffered. Proud idiots who did the least, ruled and prospered.

That was pretty good I think, I should leave it at that really. But let me add just a bit more explanation. If I was smart I could cover more in fewer words, like pithy quotes I admire. Once in a while I was inspired enough to make up a decent quote, not often though. The Bureaucracitis affected everyone in the Club to different degrees, including probably brain fog for me. I remember us Minions realizing if you wanted to drink too much, do it on a work night and just enjoy the fog at your make-work the next day. Drink less on the weekends when you wanted to get something done that you found real and meaningful.

In any case, the real output for the Club in the gigantic bureaucracy I was in, is supposed to be getting the military quality supplies and services they need, on time, and at the lowest costs we can. This requires that contractors in the private sector do the most real part of course, providing the necessary supplies and services. But buying it all capably is still a legit, necessary part, something the civilian support side should be completely devoted to doing well.

If not, our military can't do anything; it'd be the most horrible episode of *"Naked and Afraid"* ever aired. The fictitious small country of Korruptistan mentioned in Chapter 2, could walk in and kick our asses with just a small, shitty military force as our nude and desperate American forces throw rocks and sticks at them. Okay maybe plenty of them are already marching in across our southern border, and ironically we're buying them cell phones and other supplies for their mission. Sorry, couldn't help myself there.

However, most of the time and effort applied at the Club, as mentioned at the start of this I'd call it 90% of it, didn't support the end game. It impeded it. Just look backward from that real goal and think about what makes any sense towards reaching it, even from just what this book presented. Not much, I'm sorry to say.

The firm belief was controlling it all closely enough with massive amounts of continually changing coverage, every single micro-step though most of them are just manufactured, will somehow bring success. But most of what is manufactured stems from supporting every objective other than that most important objective, or is just to cover the asses of Rulers. All the political motives, we touched on that already, all the self-serving motives of so many of those allegedly in charge.

To me, everyone in the Club was making a good living, but those who played it best, who were just killing it, getting rich for being ridiculous in many cases, did so at everyone else's expense, including yours. It wasn't all of our Rulers, of course, we've been over that. But the worst of them, the proud clueless Rulers were always protected, all responsibility diluted across so many, "*When everyone is in charge no one is in charge.*" Damn, another good one there, and I don't know who coined it to give them credit.

The Club's committed and convenient belief that all its stunningly dysfunctional ways actually worked great, also meant only its Minions could fuck things up. Okay I messed up some beyond that too, have I mentioned yet how thankful I was that no one could get fired?

However, the opposite really is true of believing the madness trying to control everything, and supporting all sorts of motives other than we should have been supporting, will bring success. The real goal of supporting the military is failed the most. Also the compliance, for some reason still the most important goal for so many in Club, evidently to protect the

Rulers, just got worse as all the convoluted processes grew and grew, and the buying timeframes were of course comparable to glacial speeds. Sorry glacier fans, I know that's insulting.

"Thousands and thousands of laws brings lawlessness, endless complexity brings endless interpretations" is another good one, this seemed to be the right place to share it. No idea who originated it, either, but I cut it out of a newspaper and posted it at my desk long ago. It was removed after a while, no doubt by a proud, SADD Ruler.

Also and perhaps most importantly, the vast, complex and controlling micro-   procedures   and   the hyper-micromanagement to try to show we met it all, took us away from focusing on the steps we could do better, some actual meaningful parts. Namely buying exactly the right stuff that met the mission need, how much of it, and sending it to the right place, at the right time. We fucked that up constantly, surprisingly enough, since we were working on everything else, the focus always on what didn't matter.

Maybe the Club just got the jump on what other movements in America are up to, High Rulers totally controlling everything will bring success, including peace and prosperity for all, because they really are amazing, not one of them inept and suffering from SADD. Extremes of both main sides seem to believe in that, no one else does. Controlling what you are allowed to know, or especially what you could say, kept increasing at the Club over the years too. Maybe that was an interesting parallel.

One more good one, *"Only the gifted can understand the gifted,"* comes to mind, and to my knowledge that was mine as I assembled a bunch of fitting quotes for this book. When the gifted even just blatantly lie to you, it's for your own good. So don't worry Minions, you don't need to know otherwise.

However, what if the gifted are self-serving idiots instead, really just proud fools? Or even if not, at least no smarter than the rest of us. They still get to live really well if they pull off their dream. Not us.

Chapter 7
Top Fed Lines of Futility

"It's not just seeing the forest through the trees. They can't see it through the leaves and twigs."

An Anonymous Minion Philosopher who became a valued friend of mine early on, Circa 1994.

You could tell from what's been presented so far, that there often was a sense of futility in our ranks. Unfortunately also some frustration, even bitterness at times, as we've covered too. But the better news is we really did keep finding lots of humor in it, bonding over the dysfunction and hopelessness, finding admittedly twisted ways to enjoy it, even reaching the Celebration Stage for some of us.

So I share a top list of really good lines we found or developed over the years, in addition to using some of my favorite quotes throughout this book. A few I even originated, to the best of my knowledge, anyway.

Before we get to what the remarkable manufactured jobs phenomena adds to up in terms of its impact on you as the taxpayer, it seemed fitting to show we at least arrived at this result, also to convey a bit more on the Club Fed condition before we get into its consequences.

Also, my hunch is a pause may be in order at this point. A refreshing reset trying to help bring a sense of calm, hopefully with an added dose of amusement, before you read onward.

So without further ado, I bring you the top Club Lines I have left, since I used so many brilliant ones already:

"When you stand for nothing you fail everything..."

Another where I'd like to give appropriate credit to whoever coined it, good chance it was a Minion in reference to their Rulers.

"DoD never lies. It just changes the truth..."

I heard this wise statement from mainly Active Duty Military and Veterans early on, though I don't know its origins.

"Someone wrote down that policy, so it must be very smart..."

This was also from the Minion Philosopher mentioned at the start of this chapter, who I became friends with in my early days at the Club.

"The Cobbler's son has no shoes."

I first heard this from a Company CEO I dealt with, in regards to dealing with my agency within Club Fed.

"The experts in the work have never done the work."

To my knowledge I coined this one. I used it a bit already, but I submit it's worth a clear quote here.

"Done is better than perfect."

A great line, origins unknown to me but I ended up using it in some meetings since it tended to bring a bewildered look from my Rulers. Especially since their impossible goal was perfect surrounding documents instead of the best possible real results.

"Perfect is the enemy of the good."

Similar to the done vs. perfect line, and deployed on occasion for the same effect. I enjoyed those moments.

"The only output is more inputs to nowhere."

Another from me, I hadn't heard it before at least, and so insightful it bears repeating despite being basically the Chapter 2 title.

"No price is too high to show we accounted for a penny..."

I believe this is also mine, and admit I could be showing some SADD signs at this point. I'd submit not really though, because I can admit it.

"Denial is convenient. You don't have to do shit."

From my friend Jackie while speaking of our worst Rulers, and she also coined the one word hit *"Clownage"* mentioned in Chapter 1.

Chapter 8
Club Fed by the Numbers

"The Government isn't failing because it's too big. It's failing because it's not big enough."

Another from a Minion Happy Hour, Circa 2019

Glug, glug, glug... That's the sound my favorite bottle of bourbon made when I poured an extra- strong, jumbo sized Old Fashioned after certain days at the Club, namely when I failed to stay in the Acceptance or Celebration stages. You might want to reach for one before you continue reading.

Is it hot and sunny out, though? Then it's not as good, you could try a giant Long Island Iced Tea instead, five strong alcoholic beverages in on that one, powerful yet somehow still refreshing. Dangerous, really, don't drive with either choice. You could spill them and what a waste that would be, plus the price of them has been soaring, in no small part due to what you're about to learn of the Club's impact on you.

Well it's your call, you are who's choosing to read onward, with or without those suggested aids. Not me, don't blame me if this really hurts. You're sure then, you really want to proceed? Okay you asked for it.

(Incidentally, if you want to be spared all the build-up numbers and computations, just skip to the very end of this chapter for a succinct summary. No one could blame you for not studying how I got there. It's tedious, not that much fun, but I do try to work in a few significant stats for context, and smart ass remarks of course, always trying to lighten things up.)

So anyway, here we go on the full story of the numbers...

First, just how big is the so-called white collar welfare state of Club Fed? Again, I'm not saying there isn't a need for still a significant number of Club gigs. Just bear with me, we're talking the numbers here; there will be some analysis later.

Fittingly, no one seems to know just how many Club Fed gigs there are. The US Bureau of Labor Statistics as of November of 2022 showed it as 2,871,000 Federal employees. Brookings.edu showed the Feds had 4,100,000 employees in 2020. A U.S. Congress report at crsreports.congress.gov shows 4,308,338 employees (includes civilian and military) as of 2020, and it looked pretty credible to me. A bunch of Feds I bet reviewed that one; then again they could have fucked it up more.

However, since no one seems to really know, let's estimate it at 3,500,000, which seems fair and I'd rather err toward the low side so you don't start drinking too much as you read this. Plus it's a nice simple number; I seek out such things to counter all my years at the Club.

Next, I'm sorry to be the one to tell you that's not nearly all of the Federal employees doing a lot of the Club's work, fake shit or not, whatever the mix is. The full-time employees under contracts and grants serving the Club are about 6,800,000 according to Brookings.edu in 2020, and The.hill.com showed 5,300,000 working for the Feds under contracts and grants in 2019.

Again, who really knows, but let's estimate it at another nice simple number, 6,000,000 for purposes of this exercise, which seems pretty fair to me, not just going with the higher number.

So we're at an estimated total of 9,500,000 people working at, or for, Club Fed. On a side note, I wonder if even a fourth are Minions producing the make-work for everyone else? Okay forget I said that, strike it from the record.

The first Google hit shows 147,810,000 people employed in the U.S. in 2020. Thankfully growing since then it appears, but that means about 6.4 percent of all employment in the U.S. is with the Feds, at least pretty recently.

Make of that what you will on its own, but other context may be fitting. Let's share a few other pertinent numbers for comparison:

States, all 50 of them together, and their local governments too, total about 18,000,000 employees according to statista.com in 2021. I don't know if that includes contracted and grant gigs, but let's just leave it at that number. In researching this I found that number used several times to downplay the size of Club Fed, since it's *"only"* about half the size of all 50 of the state and local governments combined.

That's a tough sell for me. While the Club has definitely legit jobs like the active duty military and certainly others, the state and local gigs have police, firefighters, teachers, definitely still others that seem hands down very legit. There are 50 state governments out there, and countless thousands of local governments; counties, cities, townships. My gut tells me the percentage of their jobs that are without question needed, exceeds the Club's, but I'm not going there. I'm just going with the raw numbers.

Now how 'bout a couple private sector numbers.

The largest private sector employer in the U.S. according to Thehill.com in 2019 was Wal-Mart, at 1,500,000 employees, just 16% the size of Club Fed. They have a major presence in every state, seems like every decent sized town on up, and move products everywhere, every day. Supplies we all need and want for our lives; food, clothing, electronics, booze, toys, lots of other shit, plus they have booze too. They supply all this to most everyone in America it seems like.

At least everyone not using Amazon, the second largest employer in the U.S. at about 1,000,000 people according to NBC News in 2021. Maybe even more impressive than Wal-Mart, but both extraordinary in my book, just everything people across America need and want, somehow gets to them every day from Amazon. The Amazon team is call it only about 11% the size of the Federal Government, and like Wal-Mart they sure seem to do a lot, reach a lot of real results for us.

Did I mention the Federal Government employs an estimated 9,500,000 people? Sorry, I know I did. Just trying to keep things on point here, and in perspective, which includes the total Federal workforce at almost four times the size of the two largest private sector employers combined.

Bear with me in looking at a couple other comparisons, for context. The US Census Bureau in 2021 showed just 10 states with their entire known, documented population, every man, woman, child and other, with over 9,500,000 people. They are our very largest states; California, Texas, Florida, New York, Pennsylvania, Illinois, Ohio, Georgia, North Carolina and Michigan. These states are huge; I've spent time in a number of their largest cities, grew up in one of them, and oftentimes couldn't even move in the sheer gridlock of their masses. A sea of humanity everywhere it seemed like; densely populated in their urban areas as far as the eye could see.

It's easy to forget that a million is a thousand-thousand, a big number. Ten million is a hundred thousand-thousand. It's a lot of people, it really is. It's filling a giant college football stadium, like the University of Michigan's Big House in Ann Arbor, MI, a hundred times over.

Consider also that ten states, granted states at the lowest end in terms of population numbers in the U.S., but still ten states altogether, combine for a total known population of less than 9,600,000 people. These states are New Hampshire, Maine, Rhode Island, Montana, Delaware, South Dakota, North Dakota, Alaska, Vermont, and Wyoming. The Federal

Government has about the same population as all ten of these states combined; every man, woman and child in them altogether.

<u>Now you just put that down.</u> <u>Stop it. Don't start drinking that much right now, we have a ways to go here.</u>

The Federal jobs are darn good in terms of pay and benefits. I would know, it's been a very good living for me, definitely. Fedsmith.com in 2021 showed it as $90,500 for average pay, in 2022 they showed it at $143,600 for average total compensation, salary and benefits. The benefits percentage seems pretty high there; I found another hopefully credible source showing it at 36% of pay (hr.nih.gov/sites/default/files/public/documents/2022-04/total_compensation_flyer.pdf).

Ziprecruiter as of Dec 2022 showed average Federal pay at $108,600, not sure on the benefits though. Again, we don't need to be exact here, let's go with a total average estimate of $130,000 for salary and benefits, reducing the highest total number some, but recognizing the higher pay number a bit.

That's for direct Federal employees, the contracted and grant people also doing the work of the Feds, cost more. They don't necessarily get paid more; in fact it's reported to be less in many if not most cases for equivalent jobs to the Feds. But being under contract, their cost is their pay and benefits plus all the company's indirect charges and margin.

Long story, I have some significant experience in this part, and I'm here to tell you that $200,000 per year for each of them, again their actual pay averages way less, but that is probably the low end of what gets billed by the company. Like your car mechanic's rate. It's for example a $125 rate billed but the mechanic may get paid $35 an hour, and I believe most of the Fed's contracted jobs pay more than that, with much higher indirect charges than small auto repair shops. I did see that buy.gsa.gov shows a recent average of $117 per hour for contracted Federal service work across many kinds, in terms of its fully burdened contract billing rate. That is over $240,000 per year using 2,080 hours as a work-year, so using $200,000 as an estimate seems fair to me.

Okay brace yourself for this...

3,500,000 direct Fed jobs times $130,000 is $455,000,000,000.

6,000,000 contracted Fed jobs times $200,000 is $1,200,000,000,000.

We're at $1,655,000,000,000, which I think is $1.655 trillion per year as the beginning cost of the Fed's total employment. Well I didn't see this coming either, I didn't compute any numbers until I was reaching the end of this project. Also, it may not have been as noticeable over time since personnel costs are usually considered to be direct employees only, whereas the Feds employ way more full time people via contracts and grants. So their costs would be within other areas, such as an agency's acquisition spending, instead of within the agency's direct human resources.

Drink 'em if ya' got 'em. A pause inserted again here in case you do need another drink right now...like I do

Feds also need places to work, plenty still do in person, those now working remotely in most cases to my knowledge still have offices to go to as needed. The facilities and office space require at least some costs identified.

This was tougher to look into. Again I want to err toward the lower end of a given cost to deter any thought of an Insurrection if this gets out there much. It seems fair to just go with general office space costs per employee though we know there are lots of other facility costs, equipment costs, etc. But I still want to keep this simpler, so using a published average annualized cost, the one I found from 2018 is close enough, which was $18,000 per employee (www.iofficecorp.com/blog/space-management-empty-desk).

Using that workstation cost for every Fed seems excessive to me, also since so many are contracted, though a sizeable number of those are working at Federal facilities. Plus we're not including a bunch of other costs. But I meant what I said at the start of the book, I want to leave no harm, including inspiring excessive drinking or Insurrections. Arbitrary I know, but I'm just going with half the number of total Feds, 4,750,000 times $18,000 for $85,500,000,000.

So we're now at about $1.74 trillion for the annual costs of the Club, $1.655 trillion for the employees plus the $85.5 billion for their office space, or whatever facility costs per employee, which I think are understated significantly.

I'm not even going to work in the giant annual travel costs for the Club, all the trips involved. Fortunately very few, other than our Climate Czar's, are on private jets at least. Damn some of the Fed trips were really good though. My broader scene used to send a large segment of its Rulers to Orlando, FL, coincidentally every year at Spring Break, evidently the only time and place they could learn to become better Rulers together. Their families also enjoying Disney World if they went along, using the same accommodations (the rest is at their own expense if done correctly though). There was another annual winter trip to the Florida Keys for a bunch of my Rulers; I guess another location uniquely suited to honing their already fine leadership skills.

Another large cost not being accounted for here is the remarkable amount of overtime pay allegedly needed, at least in my experience at the Club. With so many positions not having true, measurable outputs to speak of, perceived extra effort could bring lots of overtime pay. Need to save up for a wedding, a big vacation, a new deck? Put in the overtime, it was encouraged where I worked much of my career. There were incredible amounts of resources, but offices still competed for who got the most jobs, with overtime being a major determining factor.

One office I was in for a long time was the most productive I had known by Club standards – the most buying actions, active contracts etc. But our team rarely worked overtime, so we ended up having to give up positions to offices which worked lots of overtime, regardless of whether or not much of anything got done there.

Anyway, there are other large, but relatively not as major costs, I'm leaving out too, like all the maintenance and security at the places we work. I looked around some but decided to leave all that out of this, for the aforementioned reasons.

However, with this massive of a Federal Government in terms of total employees working for it, one could consider the cost of at least direct Federal retirees in the equation. The sheer size of the Club brings the large number of retirees that are still on the annual bill to the taxpayer.

Here's another area where I want to stick up for the Club some, though. The retirement system we're under is not nearly the same cost to you as most other public employee systems to my knowledge. Most of us Feds are now under what is called FERS, at 1 percent per year of service to keep things simple again here. So say 35 percent of call it your pay at the end, versus at least the state and county employees I know of, who retire at twice that rate or more, though they usually aren't paid as well to begin with, I should add.

Now our Fed system is combined with Social Security when one is eligible, and something like it before you are. However, if you as a Fed don't do your part into the Fed's version of a 401K, and the Fed's part is generous, but if you don't take advantage your retirement doesn't get you very much. This I believe is part of why we couldn't get a lot of people like The Fossil to move on when they were way past eligible. They didn't put in enough of their own pay into the 401K deal. So you get to keep paying them in full until they are 75 or 85 years old in some cases, and all the remote work of recent times hasn't brought much incentive since people don't face the hassle of commuting to the office.

Incidentally I retired the first day I was eligible, I tried to help you out there. Not much consolation I know, especially since few private sector companies seem to now offer any pension at all.

Well I got off track again, but considering the annual cost of Federal retirees' pensions, let's say not with Social Security, since that is for the private sector too, you could add about $66 billion to the $1.74 trillion for current people working at the Club.

This aspect was also all over the place online too, so I again went low, using a recent fedweek.com figure of 2.2 million Federal retirees, considering contracted and grant not in on this, then times about $30,000 a year, e.g. from retirementnewsdailypress.com, since this is for pensions only, not Social Security, so the number of Fed retirees times $30,000, is around $66 billion. I didn't even include the Fed's generous portion of their retiree's health insurance premiums, again erring toward lower figures for these computations.

All in all a low end number for the cost of the total Club Fed payroll is call it about $1.8 trillion annually, to again round downward in the math. This costs every person employed in the U.S., 138,310,000 people based on the numbers presented earlier, about $13,000 each, every year, for the low end cost of the Club personnel in total, currently working and retirees.

<u>Another pause for another pour, if needed…(and you're
welcome)</u>

What was also interesting is this cost, which I'm still confident
is lower than it really is, did not seem to add up appropriately
with top level budget numbers for 2022. That showed about
$6 trillion total with 65 percent needed for Social Security,
Medicare and Medicaid, so $3.9 trillion, with then $2.1 trillion
left, and $1.8 trillion seems to use up an awful lot of that.
However, the massive Club personnel costs of administering
those programs within the Social Security Administration, the
Department of Health and Human Services (HHS), and
probably other places the way the Fed operates, would be
within the estimated total I came up with.

So there is substantial overlap across those two top level figures
of $1.8 trillion for the estimated Club total personnel tab, and
the $3.9 trillion in entitlements. I started to look into what
might get paid out in benefits vs. what those programs cost to
better identify the overlap. Then I stopped since this chapter
already had me reaching for too many strong drinks as I worked
on it, and the focus here is on arriving at mainly what
sustaining the whole Club costs annually.

Additionally, it bears mentioning again that with more of the
true total personnel costs within contract and grant spending,
it has not to my knowledge been as identifiable as direct federal
employee costs, which are less than a third of this total Fed
personnel price tag. Regardless, it really does seem like the
country is in a mega-huge shit storm of trouble taking in
around $4 trillion a year compared to all it is spending.

Please note I'm no expert at this, just a Fed retiree and concerned citizen wanting to check it out, and I'm not under oath or anything like that, either, nor am I trying to present misinformation. I invite more takes and computations, definitely. I think it's safe to say however you slice it, even if other figures are many tens of billions off from those numbers, that the cost of the whole Fed scene still is one ginormous, unsustainable train wreck.

Let me make one more comment for perspective, similar to pointing out just how big of a number 10 million people is. A trillion dollars is a thousand billion, each billion a thousand million, each million a thousand-thousand. We've grown numb to how astonishing a trillion really is, plus our schools may be focusing on teaching other more important concepts.

Well that wasn't nearly as fun as the rest of the chapters, in fact it kinda' sucked. I truly had no idea it would amount to that much. But I thought I had to try to cover it. Here's a fast review, also since I said at the start of this chapter you might want to skip to the very end to avoid some tedium, granted you missed some incidental way cool info and brilliant takes if you did:

Summing Up a Gigantic Shit Sandwich...

The total number of people working for the Federal Government is an estimated 9.5 million, directly and through contracts/grants, vs. the 50 states and all local governments combined at 18 million. The Feds are also about four times the size of the two largest U.S. private sector employers combined, Wal-Mart and Amazon, which have about 2.5 million employees in total. The *total annual price tag for the Fed personnel bill is estimated at $1.8 trillion a year as best I could tell (including a cost for Fed retirees), though sources including their significant variances in numbers warrant additional attention by whoever wants to put up with that. If reasonably in the ballpark, the total cost just to sustain all Club Fed personnel and retirees is around $13,000 annually for each and every working person in the United States. This is in addition to the almost $100,000 on every American for our staggering national debt, which is about $250,000 for every working citizen.*

So at last on this note, if you're still with me, reasonably sober and not plotting an Insurrection after taking that in, we'll get to I think some better news in the next chapter. Again, I mean to leave no harm, so don't hate on me until after you finish this book, when I think you will find no reason to.

Chapter 9
Hope for the Hopeless

"If the Club just finds the will, there's an easy way."

A modest revision of the famous "Where there's a will..." line.

The astonishingly ginormous Federal Government is far from hopeless I submit. It's definitely not entirely led by proud, SADD suffering idiots. Far from it, there are plenty of intelligent, capable Feds, lots of its Minions and even enough of its Rulers too. They have just been overwhelmed and for the most part defeated by the collective's very persistent case of Bureaucracitis.

Again, as mentioned in the prologue, I sure don't have the answers to this mess, its staggering costs to every U.S. citizen and our economy crushing the country more and more every year. However, I will offer some suggestions starting with something very easy to do if the Feds can just bring themselves to do it. No one will be harmed at all, as mentioned from the start this book tries to hurt no one. It just makes fun of plenty of people and institutions that deserve it, for the most part.

Then a few more fixes that aren't as easy, though still readily attained with just the will to execute them, even partially, and still no one has to leave the Club if they don't want to. Plus of course no harm to Federal retirees, have I mentioned yet that I'm one of those?

Incidentally, I really do appreciate you still paying me, and especially my full pay before now. In return I did spend most of it supporting people with unquestionably real jobs, and my wife and I have always been really big tippers when we went out. It's usually at least 40 percent, oftentimes way more when the tab was cheap enough, which it was where we tend to go. It always irritated me when people in the Club didn't at least do that. Leave the good people working hard for them in private sector jobs, who also arguably did more for them than vice versa, and then still had to pay their salaries, a good tip (please).

Yet I digress again. The follow-through to a fix or two is a lot like working out, as many of us already know. I know I need to do it; I just don't like it much. I like eating a chocolate donut in the morning instead, after a large hearty omelet breakfast with the trimmings, and a 32 ounce iced coffee, at least partly coffee, mainly cream though. But if I just make myself actually start the work out, I then do it easily enough, every time. It's just the will to actually start it, the rest isn't too difficult.

So let me start with a really easy way to quickly start saving hundreds of billions off the price tag of Club Fed in no time. I know it's not a novel new idea, no brilliant insight involved, just the simple way everyone knows, or should know, will work, but so far no one has had the will to execute...

<u>Make Attrition the Mission</u>

(Since you've so fucked up the rest of it)

Yes, far from an original idea but with almost 10 million Feds in the Club, again both directly and contracted, using just a modest attrition rate sensibly can shave a lot in just a little time. I'd argue no backfilling at all for a while to bring even a bigger, faster gain. That would be easy too, think just about what this book alone showed, the Club could easily absorb that if it chose to.

Okay, we know too many would see that as asking too much, and we want this to be the easiest way, plus there sure is something to say about getting new people in the game even when trying to reduce its number of players. We had lots of good people come along, unfortunately we just lost some of the very best due to pandemic Bureaucracitis. They never got to reach the Acceptance stage.

So let's look at what a 3 to 1 hiring freeze brings, hiring one new Fed for every three that leaves, and assume say a 6% attrition rate annually. That might be on the high side, it looks like 5% annually is more prevalent in online research. But indulge me, I want to apply an easy to use 4% reduction in numbers of people in the Club annually, which would impact Fed retiree numbers over time as well.

Also to keep it simple, the annual total cost of the Club from the last chapter will be used, not getting into the weeds of per employee costs including the significant difference in contracted vs. direct Feds, though contracted Fed costs being more reduced would save even more, and faster. I also won't adjust for inflation, though we know that's extra high right now in 2023. We're going to be optimistic and believe that's going to get under control before long.

A simplified take is therefore:

Year 1: $1.8 trillion x 96 percent = $1.728 trillion, savings of $72 billion

Year 2: $1.728 trillion x 96 percent = $1.658 trillion, about another $70 billion

And so on, let's say for 5 years, and the price tag is down to about $1.466 trillion, a savings of around *$334 billion*. Not bad at all for not doing that much at all, really. Just the Club being willing to, and the better part of half a trillion is easily spared.

Over 10 years, and hell yes the Club can easily sustain the hiring restrictions that bring it, the savings amount to a staggering *$605 billion,* well over half a trillion, to spare all of us some serious pain in taxes or debt, or buy lots of solar panels, whatever is decided. I guess it won't buy an electric vehicle for every U.S. household like I threw out there at the beginning of this book. But not bad either, definitely one giant booze voucher program if it'd help unite us.

Now if you're thinking the Feds can't absorb that, with no significant regulation or policy changes in their practices, just leaving its absolute and undeniable train wreck of methods alone, you really are drinking way too much right now. Please stop it. That may have been justified in the last chapter, but not now. We're on the upswing here.

Let me offer some additional explanation, in case what was covered on these pages, or your own knowledge and experience, don't already scream at you that it's true. I was among the core Minions who carried the operation where I was in DoD; the majority of the make-work that fed even more of the gigs surrounding us, gave them something to do. I know it's like that everywhere, at least in government, just bear with me here.

Practically every civilian job related to that in some way, the sort of production side being shared across all the related and supporting touches that were formulated over the years. As mentioned the military is who defends the nation, the private sector provides their needed supplies and services. Almost all the civilian jobs allegedly facilitate supporting the troops through the private sector part, ultimately via contracts, granted some may not have realized it. The massive resources established for the monstrosity of processes to buy things, also brought the disproportionately large personnel, finance and accounting, IT systems support, and other surrounding departments. The cumulative ripple effect is more like a tidal wave.

Anyway, us core Minions still had plenty of goof-off and down time on our hands, as you may have noticed in Chapter 1, often just due to waiting on assorted Rulers to let us proceed. It was great, I was living the dream, and could still easily defend that us primary Minions produced the vast majority of the make-work. Then when you think about all the Minions that wouldn't or couldn't do much, remember no one gets fired, there are no real consequences; and more importantly, all the surrounding gigs and what they allegedly did, the Feds are clearly overstaffed even for their remarkably vast, dysfunctional, manufactured practices.

Believe me, I worked in dozens of offices across DoD over 30 years, dealing with hundreds more, even some outside of DoD, enough to know many of my fellow Minions in them reasonably well, and this is absolutely true. The surrounding roles we supported were even better in terms of time on their hands; those gigs at least in my experience included the most Feds running side businesses too. I'd literally wait a week for three Rulers in just one of the review offices to share my stack of paperwork (and no others), then bestow their trifecta of wisdom upon me so I could change some things and show they contributed. We'd get a spreadsheet a month from a six-figure salary sidebar Ruler who then just tormented us for data off and on until the next month's spreadsheet. That was their whole existence other than the fake classes and other BS we all faced.

The Rulers whose full-time gigs created even more misguided micro-policies and processes for us to mess up at, lived even better. You could work on one or two of those for years, someday issuing a complete disaster that helped us fail even more to attain any real results. Then reap the rewards for it and very possibly get promoted, all of this for about 5 hours of applying yourself a week, spending the rest of your time on Facebook.

Astonishingly, those projects, and the commitment to rewarding perceived effort instead of actual results, included applying less vetting, at least much less effective vetting, than buying a bunch of office chairs. That purchase was more critical to the mission I guess, than a new policy that impacted, likely impeded, every action supposedly supporting the mission.

Well I apologize once again for getting a bit off-track there. But this time it was for a good reason, it was to offer the next couple of fixes...

Corral the Clownage

The Minion gig I had, and millions like it across the Federal Government, and even more associated with it, all directly or indirectly related to just buying stuff. That's it, and the process for that doesn't need to be so, so complicated, not at all. Certainly not to the tune of tens of thousands of disorganized and constantly changing pages of rules and procedures across dozens of different streams. Absolute chaos is believed to make our nation more secure, which then guarantees its insecurity. Anyone who believes that is necessary, and sorry to be so blunt, but they clearly are an utterly SADD idiot. Or they also work for a nation that hates ours, even secretly, maybe Korruptistan from Chapter 2.

A competent institution would use just one, comprehensive set of rules and procedures for this process, as well as any other major processes, with it being sensibly organized, even if it is overly large. The basic process in this case is just define what you need, solicit offers, even just one if no other choice. Then evaluate the offers, award a contract and see it through. That's it.

Now we know some requirements can get very involved, definitely some of DoD's needs, therefore so can evaluating proposals on them, but that's not something you can micro-script across thousands of controlling rules. You have to apply some actual meaningful work, research, identify exactly what gets the job done and what the private sector produces or can also produce, on a case by case basis. You know, the important part we mess up all the time since we focus on everything else. The vast majority of what's needed is already commercially produced anyway, not complicated at all. But newer, more involved needs also still don't benefit from a complete and total mess of micro-controls that impede them.

Nevertheless, I won't spend more time trying to explain that, the odds of it being grasped by the Highest Rulers are too low. I'm just saying take all the existing scattered chaos and compile it all into one complete set, the same sheet of music for everyone. Even just doing that will expose the ridiculous duplication and needless fine-tuning, the tiny, silly differences across the layers and related separate streams of coverage. The monstrosity will greatly benefit from that alone, even if the commitment to micro-controlling everything is maintained.

This has been proposed before, some no doubt understand it'd help immensely, but actually doing it is so daunting no one has had the will to try. But you really could get a bunch of even policy making Rulers, since we're not asking them make more dysfunctional policies, just corral all the current ones into one set for everyone, eliminating the duplication and micro-differences across streams, and pull this off.

It'd make the attrition approach way easier, definitely. Plus bring more benefits like consistency, what the Rulers insist is important, and transferability across Club gigs, not such a huge learning curve when people change jobs in the Club.

Also, allow changes to rules just once a year, in an "Open Season" fashion such as is done with Federal Health Insurance changes. A competent institution would do that in all areas it makes sense. If we got by this long without another new policy or change to it, certainly it can wait until the next open season. Who knows, you might even arrive at changes that aren't as incompetent by handling it that way, try to work smarter on them the rest of the year, and definitely implement them way better, using a more organized means, including communication and training on them. At least do that much even if you don't corral all the clownage into one set of rules, albeit still gigantic.

But speaking of clownage, here's the next suggestion...

<u>Consequences for Cluelessness</u>

Now, now, don't you worry, any of you Rulers who may be reading this; I'm not suggesting actual tough consequences at all. Again, no one would leave the Club if they don't want to, and still no one would be exposed for how much they've truly fucked things up. That will still be completely diluted and disguised, so don't fret it. But many of you would mess things up much less by this suggestion, and here's why:

The biggest reason our practices suck is because no one developing and issuing them has to execute them. They never have to battle through their own stupid methods.

If you did have to execute them as a Minion, be an actual stakeholder, they'd get a lot better, definitely. So the Club has to shift these tasks to capable Minions, the core Minions really, not the clownish ones. I know this sounds like fantasy, but it really is attainable if people have the will. The full-time policy making roles have to go, or at least be reduced, but they move into the quasi-production Minion gigs instead, helping to spread out the make-work so the most capable Minions can be who develops, or who hopefully fixes somewhat at least, the dysfunctional processes. Or if they only succeed in lessening the damage moving forward, that's a big win too.

The review Rulers should also be shifted to Minion roles, to be stakeholders in the practices. There was already some so-called peer review where I worked, but it was limited and strictly in addition to all the lanes of judgment by people who don't often understand that they're judging. If they had to take on the actual make-work, they'd understand it all much better, including the pain which can be brought by relative cluelessness getting in the way all the time. The Club can even leave them in their current gigs and assign them at least some significant make-work execution start to finish, with the same required deadlines (yes I know 1-2 years isn't very meaningful though). Then all reviews would essentially be peer reviews.

The disconnects across these review Rulers really were astounding, everyone would benefit if they gained more of a clue. I'd have someone who studied my heaps of make-work documents oftentimes way more than a week, essentially say *"You imbecile, it's all right there to follow, all you had to do on that part is use the updated DoD Instruction 5788.22 Section 417.94 Paragraph 88.7 (a) (1) (iii)..."*

They didn't understand executing even a tiny part in our practices, but more importantly, the totality of it, the absolute fact that no one could even find it all, yet alone follow it, also somehow in a way that all later interpretations would be satisfied with. Again, there really were many thousands of pages of coverage required, dozens of different streams, all of it continually changing. It made preposterous seem practical, it really did. Mere words can't do justice to how dumb that is.

Well if you thought that last offered approach was pure fantasy, despite it being very attainable if the Club was willing to, you're going to love the next one. But I'm still going to share it:

<u>Consequences for Corruption</u>

Yes, yes, just outrageous, delusional, utterly obscene! Okay we all know it won't ever happen, I'm not denying that, at least not the consequences that are truly deserved. Permanent Washington, the *"Beltway Hold 'Em"* example in Chapter 2, really was on track, the root cause of the Club's dysfunction is the corrupt legislation that starts it all. So the root cause is Congress, namely the bribery of it every single day.

An actual balanced budget requirement like their subjects...uh'... I mean constituents face in their regular lives and businesses. Members and families of Congress prohibited from owning individual stocks, meaningful strict limits on campaign and special interest donations, reigning in the bribery at least a little, all that is completely outlandish I know. Beyond blasphemous, forget I even wrote it down. Strike it from the record forever, please. None of that can happen, especially given that Congress itself would have to vote it in.

Instead, and I know this idea would have to be voted in too, but I'm offering it anyway, always hopeful, and if enough people learn of it maybe enough pressure can be applied to call 'em out, make them at least propose it and vote on it. Here it is...

The annual change in the deficit, and the annual change in the total absolutely astonishing national debt at $31 trillion and counting, determines the pay of members of Congress.

Their pay goes up or down depending on those figures going down or up, the same percentage change, or even more if it helps more. Deficit spending at another record, like fiscal year 2022's spending budget of $6 trillion vs. tax revenue of $4 trillion? That's a 33 percent pay cut for all of Congress.

Now we know the historical corruption also means many, especially the most long-standing members of Congress, don't need a Federal salary at all. They've used their gigs to build tremendous wealth with or without it, just think what inside knowledge of future massive spending on COVID vaccines brought some of these High Rulers. But the pay driver suggestion at least calls them out, hopefully shames them into ruining our lives less than they have been. They'd be forced to work across the aisle, not just say they do, while they instead dig in and blame.

It's fun to think about at least, maybe predict the headlines in late 2031...*"Welcome to the CBS evening news. Beginning next January, Members of Congress will be paid a salary of $780 per year..."*

They deserve it, granted other high ranking Beltway Bandits do too. Every American owes nearly $100,000 and counting thanks to the total irresponsibility, gross negligence and corruption that's gone on for decades. One can't single out the current administration though they sure have done their share. *We the people* are paying the consequences, not these High Rulers. Luckily for them, though, too many people don't understand they are paying for it every day, becoming poorer every day, their life savings getting crushed too. Paying just the interest on our national debt exceeds the annual budgets of nearly all other countries, with just 15 other countries spending more than we spend on interest alone (per a recent Wikepedia.org ranking of countries by annual budget).

Besides the stupendous financial failure we all get punished for, we pay not just from our livelihoods, we have to put up with all the dysfunction it brings, Fed Minion or not. In a way all of us have become Minions serving their Rulers in Government, it impacts everything we do, increasingly controlling us more and more every year.

Just think about it. Besides clearly not knowing how many employees the Club even has, their own lanes differing so greatly in the numbers as discussed in Chapter 8, no one even knows how many agencies and departments Club Fed has. It has grown so much over the years, with many of them making more rules and policies impacting us.

Seven different Federal sources online show the current count of Federal Agencies ranged from 115 to 443, absolutely no one even knows. No fucking clue. Different Federal offices within all those, how many thousands in total for the unknown hundreds of Federal agencies and nearly 10 million employees? No one has any idea at this point, and truly accounts for their costs (these figures from forbes.com, 7/05/2017):

Administrative Conference of the United States – 115 agencies shown

FOIA.gov – 252

2016 Federal Register Index – 272

Regulations.gov – 292

United States Government Manual – 316

Federal Register Agency List – 440

USA.gov - 443

I bet you could throw a bunch of bureaucratic words in a hat, pull some out, and it exists as a Federal Agency or Department. Wait, let me try that...yes we do have a U.S. Department of Ancillary Evaluation of Pre-Existing Analysis and Assessments. It has maybe 600 Club members but no one really knows.

So many agencies and offices can be eliminated entirely, no doubt. If we existed better before them, why have them? No one has a clue how many, or accountability for what it all costs. But you'd better have your shit perfectly together if you face an IRS audit.

Pure fantasy again, but how 'bout this anyway – since members of Congress seem mostly wealthy with or without their Federal salaries, *at least apply the same fiscal incentive to Agency and Department Heads.* Spend 10% more this year, Mr. Secretary of Redundant Redundancy Studies? Enjoy your 10% pay cut. Or why not save 5% and enjoy a raise instead?

All in all, a competent and responsible permanent Washington would never have let it come to this, not even close. We wouldn't be tabling any of this, wouldn't even have to think of it. As a fan of history, granted reading mostly historical fiction but also plenty of non-fiction, quite a few past civilizations would have executed their Rulers long before it got to this. I just read about it in an account of ancient Greek Athens.

Please forget I said that - no one is suggesting any Rulers get harmed other than maybe pay incentives. No one wants an Insurrection in any way, shape or form, or massive booze handouts even if they sound tempting. That was just sharing a part of human history, nothing more.

Well I'd better wrap this chapter up, so I'll leave you with this:

Is Club Fed too big to fail? Or is it too big to succeed?

We all know it's both. There really still is hope though, and it'd be easy to make a huge positive difference. It just takes the will to.

Chapter 10
To My Fellow Fed Faithful

Wow, a chapter starting without a way cool quote! I could have used one, I do have more I didn't get in. If nothing else, I'm pretty good at being a smart ass. But I wanted to mix things up, keep you guessing.

In this chapter I'd like to salute, also encourage, my fellow Minions in the Club, and the good Rulers out there too (all five of you...nah' we know it's at least ten or more). Plus I want to speak not just to where I've worked in the Club, but to whoever reads this throughout the entire Federal Government, including its contractors working for the Club. Okay that might end up being just ten or twenty people, we will see.

By now some readers might be thinking, *"Well you've mocked and insulted the shit out of us throughout an entire book. So up yours, asshole."*

Well I may not have pulled it off, but I wanted to only make fun of those who deserve it, no one else. I tried to also get the point across that not all the Club gigs are fake, a substantial amount of it is real and necessary, at a minimum portions of it, as we try to battle through the rest. Plus I really do think highly of the vast majority of the fellow Minions I've known, and quite a few Rulers as well. By extension I see the broader scene the same way, valuing teammates I've never known too, a sense of Fed unity in my view.

I sincerely tried to leave no true harm, and I think I did okay on that note. I sincerely wanted to make a positive difference too, get a message across that I want to believe could help bring meaningful change someday, which also brings me to my words of encouragement to the Club in this chapter.

Our Fed jobs really are great if you ask me, we're blessed to have them, including the incredible work/life balance they give us, and I won't reiterate too much of that. We've been over it, especially in the second two Assimilation Stages presented in Chapter 5.

Therefore if you ask me, we still owe the Club and ourselves a sincere effort to do our jobs well, even if a bunch of it is fake shit. I tried to do that, and eventually did reach some job satisfaction in accomplishing something legitimate for the military here and there. You'll hear a bit more on that shortly.

Plus in a way, such a huge struggle to get anything done, including all kinds of pushback from assorted Rulers, can really mean you accomplished more to get something done, at least overcame more. I think there's some satisfaction in that too.

So I ask you to think about that no matter how discouraging your gig may seem at times. I didn't always succeed at keeping the best attitude, as I mentioned earlier too. But when I did, no matter how utterly ridiculous things got, I was still pretty darn happy at my job, and very thankful for it.

All in all, and yes much of this has already been said so I'll just summarize here, but I'd say absolutely use the great Club Fed life to help attain satisfaction and fulfillment outside of it; the means to live a good, purposeful life. But you can get some of that on the job too, I'd say no matter what if you apply yourself to it, and we all know that's what makes us like our jobs. Or at least not hate them, not even close if you do your best to maintain the right outlook.

Let me bid my fellow Club faithful farewell with literally the email I sent to my fellow Minions, and some good Rulers, on my very last day at the Club. I think it fits here, or maybe I just share it because I thought it was some pretty good shit. Granted it's too long, since only truly smart people learn how to say more in fewer words. I don't qualify for that, so here it is:

"Teammates and Friends!!

Well this is it, today I'm signing off for good, moving onto my next chapter. Tried to keep it quiet because a broad public email thing is not for me, and neither are obligatory speeches while eating cake...knowing some in attendance may see my retirement as my first ever act of public service!

So this is being sent using the BCC feature just to some friends, and some teammates I didn't necessarily know as well, or for very long in some cases, but thought highly of and enjoyed knowing along the way. My hunch is most or all of you may have been on the same page as me – definitely appreciating our great gigs and co-workers while also finding the establishment to maybe be a complete mental insti'...uh'...well let me just characterize it as an institution offering unique procedural and leadership challenges!

In any case, thank you! I genuinely just want to say thank you, to each and every one of you reading this. I will sincerely miss all of you as well, understanding that realistically, I won't be seeing or talking to many of you again. That part of this move to my next chapter I have to say is a real bummer. But one of the only parts that is!

I want you to know that I have really, really appreciated all the good times, the fun talks, emails and laughs shared, even just the funny looks and other signs of knowing what we faced together, as we dealt with the...um'... intriguing complexities involved in getting something done now and then, or just dealing with a typical bureaucratic day. Every one of those times lifted my spirits, put a smile on my face, and made my often ridiculous days of make-work something I truly enjoyed the vast majority of the time!

Despite my past complaints about the establishment, and I do believe it...offers considerable organizational improvement opportunity...I'm very grateful for it too. What a fantastic living it has provided for my family and I, while letting me enjoy all sorts of ME time as well! It has also set up even more great outdoors living for the rest of my days. I have no idea why my wife, my adult kids and grandkids put up with me, but I'm sure thankful they do. I'll have more time than ever to test their patience! I will support some good causes too, have to pay forward the blessings (or at least reduce my taxes).

But you, my friends and teammates, are what helped me through all the times I unfortunately let myself get discouraged by the DoD scene, okay even just flat out pissed off! In retrospect I of course shouldn't have. Such a truly great gig, regardless, and I definitely move on in peace and gratitude. However, let me try to sum up an example of an aggravation I won't miss, but mainly to say that valued Homies like you are what got me through the...let's say advanced DoD resiliency training...without losing my mind (not completely at least).

So while handling hundreds of often messed up contracts over the years, I pulled off quite a few unprecedented acquisition feats for our activity, and of course through our totally f'd u'... I mean very challenging, methods. A bunch of them were first time nationwide and worldwide enterprise projects start to finish, and they'd get impeded by people, including certain leaders, throughout the journeys, plus I'd have to cover for others who inexplicably got to opt out of their part.

Quite a few players would display a bewildering combination of impressive confidence while not revealing the impressive competence behind it, presumably out of modesty. Yet somehow they were still seemingly too...let me say cautious...to do or support anything. I'd always find a way in spite of it, we have to take the risks and occasionally reach some form of result or all our jobs don't have an arguably legitimate existence.

Then other people, or even some of the same, would inevitably find supposedly serious yet essentially meaningless procedural violations, and the major successes were then deemed major compliance failures. Adding to the intrigue was some who deemed the projects failures were the same people who pile even more onto the vast mountains of processes that seem to guarantee everything will be wrong according to something or someone. They've never had to execute through the tangled labyrinth they help create but they know it works flawlessly.

Yet still after that, I'd be told to write up what returned to being major mission successes and their large cost savings, for the appraisals of some of the same people who impeded the projects and deemed them failures, since the big successes were instead now because of them!

Sorry, had to share one last example of a DoD phenomenon I won't greatly miss. But I sure can't feel sorry for myself either. Some modest flak over the years for how I'd resist the regime, which admittedly wasn't often in the smartest ways. But no major punishment for getting something done now and then, with the many positives absolutely outweighing it.

Plus I was not alone - all of us who produce some form of work product often fail at it according to those in DoD who fervently believe they are experts in what they've never done. Some of us arrived at a fitting term for it – FU, for Failure University. Many of us at least at some point are faithful students of FU making teammates look better through our failures.

So to those in DoD who don't appreciate us flunkies getting things done in spite of their methods and that their jobs need too, all I have to say is you're welcome...and FU!

Okay I'm being ridiculous but it seemed fitting as I conclude my DoD days. Also fitting because when I had the right attitude, all was maniacally funny and not infuriating thanks to great teammates like you helping me see it that way. When I did still get discouraged...well I also eventually realized it was easy to blame others for my own faults in dealing with whatever setbacks I faced. There are always plenty of ways to handle anything better, especially the best attitude to apply, and I was a slow learner on that for too long.

So yes, DoD has been not only been a great living while having fun at it, but it helped me help myself too. I truly wish those I battled with the very best as well, indeed most are decent people even if some are oblivious. They sincerely don't realize their ways block getting done what everyone needs to get done. But at least they help the rest of us experience a sense of accomplishment when we do get something done!

Well alas I conclude my final DoD email, and I wanted to send it just to those I've liked the most (the rest just get a smart-ass out-of-office). So thank you again. For everything. This email understates how much I've valued your friendship, fellowship, help and especially laughs along the way! It meant more than my words can really say here. You kept my DoD days fun, happy...and sane!

My very best fishes to you and yours always...and stay sane my friends!! "

- Jo-Jo

Epilogue

"America is the land of the free...to live within countless thousands of laws and regulations controlling your life, and forfeit a big chunk of your income for it."

Okay I made this one up too, but likely another line or two inspired it along the way.

When I began this project, the goal was to deliver a message on massive U.S. Government dysfunction and waste, at least the parts of it I learned about over more than three decades deep in the trenches of probably the absolute mother of all bureaucracies; the huge, tangled civilian empires within the U.S. Department of Defense. The objective wasn't just to raise awareness, which can make a positive difference by itself. Proposed solutions, or at least significant ways to help, were to be offered as well.

Hopefully I did a decent job of trying to reach those objectives, if enough people read this book. I do think at least 20 copies will be sold...what I'll buy for family and friends. Time will tell.

Toward trying to accomplish something with this project, reach more people and maybe some offered fixes getting noticed, I thought the book had to be funny, hard hitting, have some real attitude to it. All in all a quick fun read people don't have to go out of their way to take in. Price it low too, about the cost of a decent hamburger so more people may grab a copy.

You can read it in one evening, no problem, and hopefully get some laughs out of it at a minimum, maybe enjoy a few select beverages while you're at it. But I hope it brought some useful information too, including possible additional insight into why our Federal Government is like it is.

I really didn't plan to use as much fucking profanity as I did. Too much of that is definitely not the mark of a smart person. It loses its effect, just like too many words overall do, in my opinion. Well I already told you I'm not very smart, so I should get a pass on that. But I was trying for the right amount of foul language to bring some attitude, and it all really did come from the gut, inspired by truly giving a shit about what I was presenting.

We will know soon enough how the book is received, the message being sent, how it was delivered in hopefully not too drawn out of a way, and with a hard hitting, funny style.

I have another goal for this book I touched on in the Prologue, to support my favorite cause in retirement, the Tunnel-2-Towers Foundation which supports the families of fallen heroes of our military and law enforcement, as well as those living with severe, permanent disabilities stemming from their sacrifice for their country and communities.

Check it out sometime if you haven't already. I tried to thoroughly before I began donating to them a few years ago, and really did find them to be sincere, totally legit and dedicated, absolutely. Almost all of what they take in goes directly to their cause, which you won't find with quite a few other charitable organizations if you look closely.

If by chance this book sells enough copies, it'd be a tremendous accomplishment to pay off, or at least greatly help pay off, the mortgage of at least one family who lost a parent in the line of duty for their country or town. I'd be absolutely thrilled, the thought already brings tears to my eyes I shit you not (at least I didn't say I fucking shit you not, just now). Then again maybe this book will raise barely enough to buy a new screen door for a house the rest of the donations get to pay off, or its doorknob. Again, we'll see.

The 50% or more of author royalties will be fully accounted for, documented with the Tunnel-2- Towers Foundation, and made available to whomever else down the road. This is also since the records will be needed for at least a few of the 87,000 new IRS agents it seems we are adding to the mere 9.5 million people we already have working for the Club.

An extra interesting aspect of this project is while I wanted to get my message out on Government waste including possible causes and remedies; I didn't plan to sound as political as I know plenty of it did. It just sort of happened on its own, as the parallels with what I experienced in the Club, to what is going on in the country, became more and more apparent as I reflected on my long career of floundering around in strictly controlled make-work, and how the DoD organizations were run.

I'd better not get too started on that note, maybe another book someday if this does okay though. I already thought of GLAD – Group Lack of Awareness Disorder, and I'll share just one quick example here.

When the culture hit an all-time low in the general area I was in for the largest part of my career, an employee survey turned out to be very embarrassing for our High Rulers, possibly the very worst score in all of DoD for that organizational measure.

The short version of this intriguing story was that our Rulers, not all but the core few in power, were 100% convinced it could not have even remotely been due to their actions, our methods, absolutely anything other than the Minions. In their view we were clearly yet just by coincidence, the worst group of Minions ever assembled in DoD, though they hired us too, by the way. The core Rulers genuinely believed there was a Minion conspiracy to bring them down including Minions coordinating their survey responses together, and they launched quasi-investigations afterwards to find out who led the perceived uprising. But the truth is no one had even talked about it at all other than making fun of such things as usual, though we did then enjoy mocking how delusional they seemed to be later, their group SADD effect.

So maybe like we see happening in a broader sense for a good while now, including before the current administration. The Rulers in power can't possibly be doing anything wrong, absolutely no way could that remotely be conceivable, and any indication that they are could only be from conspiracies, misinformation, and whatever else, anything but them. Always attack and even censor or cancel whoever questions or pushes back; accuse them of the very wrong, destructive things you are the one doing. Don't ever pause to reflect on your own ways since by rule, the worst Rulers can't ever be wrong.

Well since in the end, I couldn't help myself from trying to send a broader message, let me conclude this project with what might be a funny, hopefully effective, little parable that could bring things home both to the Club Fed faithful, and everyone else too, since we're all paying for it.

One last funny anecdote I hope, but with a message of course. Credit for this idea goes to my good friend and former boss Sam. Then as usual my twisted mind took it and ran with it...

<u>Official Certified Restaurant Assistant Program (O-CRAP)</u>

So Congress comes up with a new innovative idea to help America, and maybe the world eventually, and as usual no one reads the legislation. It gets passed immediately since it was deemed another emergency need we didn't know we had until someone decided it was so.

The economic development initiative is to help eligible small start-up restaurant businesses, coincidentally in the districts of some powerful High Rulers in Congress. But instead of just subsidizing the restaurants, the legislation mandates by law that residents within 10 miles of them, must go there for a meal at least once a week. The law includes that each resident must spend at least $25 on their once a week visit. The new program is celebrated also for it not needing federal funds at all; no tax dollars are necessary, very innovative indeed.

The food and service at the O-CRAP Diners starts out okay, but prices are already very high, maybe five times higher than regular restaurants the demand is so high from the mandated visits. This was also since the restaurants had to follow additional regulations a dozen government agencies required to maintain eligibility for the program, formulated by people who haven't operated restaurants. Then the food and service get bad quickly too, their procedures didn't start well and got worse, nothing was competently organized before the launch.

Yet people keep coming, they have to or it's a misdemeanor with a fine for a first offense. It soon becomes a felony if you don't support the mandated restaurant support requirement, do your fair share to help support your community. In no time the minimum $25 visit gets you just a small, synthetic, ground beef hamburger, nothing else. They're really bad too, and people are already complaining that the O-CRAP burgers taste like shit.

The area residents aren't happy at all about the new law requiring they support the new diners, but they have to go. The money keeps pouring in, and they provide worse and worse food and service since people have no choice but to keep paying for it. It doesn't take long until the $25 minimum needs to be raised by an amended law to $50, but the O-CRAP Diners still get worse. They get to succeed in spite of themselves, how they operate gets more dysfunctional the more they try to do. Yet the money keeps flowing in even if they just sprinkle some rabbit shit on an O-CRAP plate, for something plant-based, organic and healthy you can get for the $50 minimum.

Meanwhile, Congress can see their O-CRAP initiative is working absolutely great, no doubt one of the best pieces of legislation to help the American economy ever implemented. The restaurants are found to be a complete success, they employ more and more people, even just to serve up some crappy shit in their messed up practices. Awards and recognition are also presented to the diners that made it such a huge win

The Rulers of the O-CRAP Diners, their owners and managers, are earning big salaries, even the cooks, wait staff; all the Minion types are getting paid very well too. Wages keep going up and so does employment in the affected areas. Inflation keeps rising rapidly since the initiative uses up a lot of labor and other resources without producing much. But no biggie, given all the other successes.

The innovative program is so successful, at least according to Congress and other prominent High Rulers in Government, that it must be expanded. These restaurants must be opened everywhere, it'd be just plain stupid not to. Yet some misguided, ungrateful fools still push back, including headlines such as *"Why O-CRAP Stinks"* and *"O-CRAP in Your Own Pants"* from cities and states that don't want it. But the High Rulers and Congress know better, and they work with their donors to limit that misinformation. They got this, no worries, and it'll just keep getting better and better. You'll see.

And maybe that's what always happens when people have no choice but to keep paying more and more for getting less and less. Okay I'm finally done now.

Acknowledgments

First I must thank my wonderful spouse, for putting up with my insanity throughout this project and in general, and for her wise take and advice on the manuscript. She's a Club retiree now too, and no one worked harder for the Feds, believe me, and whether or not she was allowed to reach any real results (and she still did, definitely).

Next, to my Homies, the fellow Minions and good Rulers, who both inspired and helped me, while at the Club but also a number of these valued friends who I sought out on this project. Too many to list, great pals like Dante, Sam, Roberto, Zeng, Jonny, Kanee, Matthias, Mayhem, Watts; I could go on and on, and am of course not using actual names here. Most still work at the Club.

I want to separately also thank four of my much appreciated Homies for their very wise review and advice on the manuscript itself – Jackie, Erika, Katrina and Nat. Invaluable takes, perspective and assistance, absolutely. With my wife that means five of the very most people-smart people I know are women. There's a takeaway there. I'm not sure what it is, I'm not smart enough because I don't identify as a woman.

My thanks also to Nat for just killing it on the book cover, so good it could well be the only reason anyone picks up a copy of the book.

Thanks to Draft-2-Digital for everything they did to make this possible. What a great service for this first-time self-published book author.

My sincere thanks also to Tunnel-2-Towers for all they do for others, as previously mentioned. Such a worthy cause, which helped give me an additional important cause to support with this project.

And finally, my heartfelt thanks to anyone and everyone who bought this book and read it. It's an honor and much appreciated. Even if the proceeds ultimately bring just $5 to Tunnel-2-Towers and that same amount for me to get two chicken burritos at Taco Bell, I am grateful.

J.J.

About the Author

Jo-Jo "J.J." Suff is the pen-name of the anonymous author, a retired U.S. Department of Defense Contracting Officer who has had articles published in Defense News, Federal Times, and a National Contract Management Association magazine. He's also had over 200 articles published on other topics, primarily his outoor pursuits. A minimum of half the author proceeds from his books support the Tunnel-2-Towers Foundation. He lives in the Great Lakes Region of the United States with his wife, in a remote, undisclosed location.

About the Publisher

This book is self-published by JJ Suff.